I0435144

Jarvis Island National Wildlife Refuge

Draft Comprehensive Conservation Plan and Environmental Assessment

Prepared by:
Pacific Remote Islands National Wildlife Refuge Complex
Box 50167
Honolulu, Hawaii 96850
(800) 792-9550

August 2007

Jarvis Island National Wildlife Refuge
Draft Comprehensive Conservation Plan
and
Environmental Assessment
Unincorporated U.S. Territory, Central Pacific Ocean

Type of Action: Administrative

Lead Agency: U.S. Department of the Interior, Fish and Wildlife Service

Responsible Official: Ren Lohoefener, Regional Director

For Further Information: Donald Palawski, Refuge Manager
                           Pacific and Remote Islands NWR Complex
                           Box 50167
                           Honolulu, HI 96850
                           (808) 792-9550

Abstract: Jarvis Island National Wildlife Refuge (Jarvis) is located in an extremely remote area of the equatorial Central Pacific Ocean. This remote location creates extreme planning and management bottlenecks in terms of ship transportation availability to access Jarvis and the operational support needed to carry out comprehensive conservation. Four conservation plan alternatives, including a Preferred Alternative and a No Action Alternative, are described, compared, and assessed for Jarvis. Alternative A is the No Action Alternative, as required by the National Environmental Policy Act. The selection of Alternative A would adopt and continue current refuge management practices conducted during short staff visits (i.e. 1 to 2 days) at approximately 2-year intervals. Management activities described in Alternatives B, C, and D progressively increase the scale and scope of management activities described in the No Action Alternative. Alternatives C and D describe desired improvements over current management that enhances protection of wildlife through increased surveillance, enforcement, monitoring, restoration, and other measures. While Alternatives C and D outline conservation measures that would be desirable from a comprehensive conservation perspective, it is beyond the current logistical realm of the U.S. Fish and Wildlife Service (Service) and financially unachievable during the lifespan of this plan (15 years). Therefore, Alternative B is the preferred alternative and describes improvements over current management that could be implemented until such time that management activities described in Alternatives C or D can be implemented. The four alternatives are summarized below:

Alternative A – No Action – This alternative assumes continuation of current management programs and is considered the base from which to compare the action alternatives.

Alternative B – Preferred Alternative -This alternative describes a modest increase in the frequency of staff visits to Jarvis but does not alter the scale or scope of the management activities.

Alternative C – This alternative provides increased frequency and duration of staff visits to Jarvis, and moderately increases scale and scope of management activities conducted during staff visits.

Alternative D – This alternative describes substantial increases to the scale, scope, and duration of management activities conducted during staff visits.

Public access to Jarvis will remain closed under all CCP alternatives. Specific requests to access Jarvis will regulated on a case-by-case basis through issuance of Special Use Permits. There are no proposed changes to the refuge boundary under any of the alternatives. The selected alternative would be used to guide refuge management throughout the life of the CCP (15–year period)

Reader's Guide

Consistent with requirements of the National Wildlife Refuge System Administration Act, as amended (16 U.S.C. 668dd-668ee), the U.S. Fish and Wildlife Service (Service) would manage Jarvis Island National Wildlife Refuge (Jarvis) in accordance with an approved Comprehensive Conservation Plan (CCP). The CCP provides long-range guidance for refuge management through its vision, goals, and objectives. No change in refuge size, boundaries, or public access and use is proposed for any alternative. The CCP also provides a basis for a long-term adaptive management process including implementation, monitoring progress, evaluating, adjusting and revising the CCP accordingly. Additional step-down planning would be required prior to implementation of certain programs and projects.

This document combines a draft Comprehensive Conservation Plan and an Environmental Assessment (CCP/EA). The following summaries are provided to assist readers in locating and understanding the various components of this combined document.

Chapter 1: Introduction, Purpose and Need for Action includes the regional context; establishment of and purposes for Jarvis; vision and goals for future management; major planning issues, concerns and opportunities identified by refuge staff, Federal, State and local agencies, and the general public; and policy for, guidance for, purpose of, and need for a CCP.

Chapter 2: Alternatives, Objectives, and Strategies describes four management alternatives including the Preferred Alternative. Each alternative represents a potential comprehensive conservation plan for the refuge. Alternative A (No Action) describes the current management of the refuge. Alternative B, the Preferred Alternative, is the proposed Draft CCP for Jarvis. Alternatives C and D describe progressively more intensive management activities if substantially greater financial resources were available for future implementation. This chapter identifies the objectives and strategies the refuge will use to meet overall goals. It also compares all alternatives and identifies those eliminated from detailed consideration.

Chapter 3: Affected Environment describes the existing physical and biological environment, public use, cultural resources, and socioeconomic conditions. This chapter represents the current baseline conditions for the comparisons and 15-year projections made in Chapters 2 and 4.

Chapter 4: Environmental Consequences assesses and projects, over the 15-year period, the affect of each alternative on the resources, programs and conditions outlined in Chapter 3 as they relate to Jarvis. Most impacts would have a positive effect on refuge fish and wildlife populations and their habitats. Mitigation and other measures are evaluated for all other avoidable consequences.

Chapter 5: Consultation and Coordination with Others provides details on public involvement and interagency coordination during the planning process.

Appendix A: Glossary of Terms and Acronyms contains a list of abbreviations, acronyms, and terms that may be unfamiliar to the reader.

Appendix B: Species Lists of Corals, Fish, Vegetation and Birds lists wildlife observed in the refuge.

Appendix C: List of Cited References provides complete bibliographic references for the citations in this document.

Appendix D: Quarantine Protocol for Jarvis Island describes mandatory precautions for visitors to protect island and marine habitats from inadvertent introduction of alien and invasive species and hazardous materials.

Appendix E: Plan Implementation and Costs includes the Refuge Operations Needs Summary (RONS) and Service Asset Maintenance Management System (SAMMS), which briefly describes projects and costs associated with the Preferred Alternative.

Appendix F: Wilderness Review for Jarvis Island NWR is required as part of this CCP. This appendix lists the criteria used in conducting the wilderness review. Jarvis appears to meet all the criterion for wilderness designation as defined by the Wilderness Act of 1964.

Appendix G: Statement of Compliance for Implementation of the Jarvis Island National Wildlife Refuge Comprehensive Conservation Plan describes the executive orders and legislative acts that apply to this CCP.

Table of Contents

Chapter 1: Introduction, Purpose, and Need for Action

1.1 Introduction

This document is a draft Comprehensive Conservation Plan and draft Environmental Assessment (CCP/EA) for Jarvis Island National Wildlife Refuge (Jarvis). Once finalized, the CCP would guide management of refuge operations, site visitation, and habitat restoration for the 15-year life of the plan. Guidance within the CCP would be in the form of goals, objectives, strategies (Chapter 1.7 and 2.6), and wilderness study findings (Appendix F). The CCP will be accompanied by an appropriate NEPA document. The final CCP will be revised as appropriate based upon public comments. The proposed action can be one of the alternatives in this draft CCP/EA, a combination of the identified alternatives, or a new alternative derived from substantive public comment. This draft CCP/EA evaluates and compares four alternatives containing programs for habitat management and restoration, ecological monitoring and research, and environmental education. It also identifies the effects of restoration and visitor use on key physical, biological, social, and cultural resources. The refuge manager of the Pacific Remote Islands National Wildlife Refuge Complex (Remotes Complex) in Honolulu, Hawaii, is responsible for implementing the approved CCP.

1.2 Purpose and Need for the Comprehensive Conservation Plan

1.2.1 Proposed Action

The Service proposes to adopt and implement a CCP for Jarvis. This draft CCP/EA evaluates and compares four alternatives and their effects on key physical, biological, social, and cultural resources. The Service has identified Alternative B as the preferred alternative because it achieves refuge purposes, vision, goals, and objectives; contributes to the National Wildlife Refuge System (System) mission; addresses issues and relevant mandates; and is consistent with sound principles of fish and wildlife management.

The alternative ultimately selected and described in the final CCP will be determined, in part, by the comments received on the draft CCP/EA. The proposed action in the final CCP may or may not modify the proposed action presented in this draft CCP/EA.

1.2.2 Purpose and Need

Overall, all refuges must comply with the System mission, goals, and policies, as described in or promulgated by the National Wildlife Refuge System Administration Act of 1966 (NWRS Administration Act), as amended (16 U.S.C. 668dd-668ee). The National Wildlife Refuge System Improvement Act of 1997 amended the NWRS Administration Act. According to the NWRS Administration Act, a CCP is required to identify and describe refuge purpose(s), habitats and wildlife, archaeological and cultural values, administrative and visitor facilities, management challenges and their solutions, and opportunities for compatible wildlife-dependent recreation. The recreational activities referenced in the NWRS Administration Act as receiving special consideration during planning efforts include hunting, recreational fishing, wildlife observation, interpretation, environmental education, and photography.

The purpose of this CCP is to develop a vision, goals, and objectives for Jarvis, which in turn provide guidance to identify and implement management activities, or strategies, during the next 15 years. Specifically, the CCP:

- sets a long term vision;
- establishes wildlife and habitat management goals and objectives;
- establishes goals and objectives for compatible wildlife-dependent recreational and educational uses;
- identifies strategies for habitat enhancement and restoration projects;
- describes the highest monitoring and research priorities; and
- describes and evaluates wilderness values.

1.3 Description of Planning Process

The CCP development process follows applicable policies contained within the Service's Fish and Wildlife Manual (Part 602 FW2.1, November 1996; Part 601 FW1, Part 603 FW1, and Part 605 FW1, June 2006), and the Wilderness Act of 1964 with respect to wilderness study and review. This Draft CCP/EA is intended to meet the dual requirements of compliance with the NWRS Administration Act and the National Environmental Policy Act (NEPA). Both the NWRS Administration Act and NEPA require the Service to actively seek public involvement in the preparation and adoption of environmental and conservation documents and policies. Furthermore, NEPA also requires the Service to consider a reasonable range of alternatives including its Preferred Alternative and the "No Action" alternative; the latter defined as continuation of current management practices.

1.4 Legal and Policy Guidance

Jarvis and its management and administrative activities are managed as part of the NWRS or System within a framework provided by legal and policy guidelines. The refuge is guided by the mission and goals of the NWRS, the purpose of the refuge as described in its acquisition authority, Service policy, Federal laws and executive orders, and international treaties.

Supplemental guidance documents (e.g., resource plans) are also included in making management decisions but cannot replace or be in conflict with the purposes for which the refuge was established or the mission of the System. Following is a discussion of concepts and guidance for the System covered in the NWRS Administration Act, Service policies, and relevant supplemental guidance documents.

1.4.1 The U.S. Fish and Wildlife Service

Jarvis is managed by the Service, within the U.S. Department of the Interior. The Service is the primary Federal entity responsible for conserving and enhancing the Nation's fish and wildlife populations and their habitats. Although the Service shares this responsibility with other Federal, State, tribal, local, and private entities, the Service has specific trust resource responsibilities for migratory birds, threatened and endangered species, certain anadromous fish, certain marine mammals, coral reef ecosystems, wetlands, and other special aquatic habitats. The Service also has similar trust responsibilities for the lands and waters it administers to support the conservation and enhancement of all fish and wildlife and their associated habitats.

1.4.2 National Wildlife Refuge System

President Theodore Roosevelt established Pelican Island, Florida as the first national wildlife refuge in 1903. Since that time, the number of refuges has expanded to include 545, totaling approximately 100 million acres. These refuges, found in every United State and several U.S. Territories, are administered collectively as a national system of lands with the specific mandate of managing for "wildlife first". This System is the largest collection of lands specifically managed for fish and wildlife conservation in the Nation and perhaps the world. The "wildlife first" mandate of the System means the needs of wildlife and their habitats take priority on refuges, in contrast to other public lands that are managed for multiple uses. The following is a description of some of the most relevant acts and policies that guide the management of the System.

National Wildlife Refuge System Administration Act of 1966, as amended
The NWRS Administration Act defines a unifying mission for all refuges, including a process for determining compatible uses on refuges, and requiring that each refuge be managed according to a CCP. The NWRS Administration Act expressly states that wildlife conservation is the priority of System lands and that the Secretary shall ensure that the biological integrity, diversity, and environmental health of refuge lands are maintained. Each refuge must be managed to fulfill the specific purposes for which the refuge was established and the System mission. The first priority of each refuge is to conserve, manage, and if needed, restore fish and wildlife populations and habitats according to its purpose. The Service has statutory authority under the NWRS Administration Act to regulate activities that occur on water bodies "within" a refuge. The NWRS Administration Act requires a CCP be completed for each refuge and that the public has an opportunity for active involvement in plan development and revision. It is Service policy that each CCP is developed in an open public process.

National Wildlife Refuge System Mission and Goals and Purposes (601 FW1)
In July 2006, the Service issued a policy (601 FW 1) which included the NWRS mission statement and NWRS goals, and described how refuge purposes are determined.

The NWRS Administration Act established the following statutory mission for the System:

> "The mission of the System is to administer a national network of lands and waters for the conservation, management, and where appropriate, restoration of the fish, wildlife, and plant resources and their habitats within the United States for the benefit of present and future generations of Americans."

The administration, management, and growth of the System are guided by the following goals (601 FW 1, July 2006)...."

- Conserve a diversity of fish, wildlife, and plants and their habitats, including species that are endangered or threatened with becoming endangered.
- Develop and maintain a network of habitats for migratory birds, anadromous and interjurisdictional fish, and marine mammal populations that is strategically distributed and carefully managed to meet important life history needs of these species across their ranges.
- Conserve those ecosystems, plant communities, wetlands of national or international significance, and landscapes and seascapes that are unique, rare, declining, or underrepresented in existing protection efforts.
- Provide and enhance opportunities to participate in compatible wildlife-dependent recreation (hunting, fishing, wildlife observation and photography, and environmental education and interpretation).
- Foster understanding and instill appreciation of the diversity and interconnectedness of fish, wildlife, plants, and their habitats.

Lastly, the NWRS Administration Act describes refuge purposes, and how these guiding principals for the refuge are located and documented.

Appropriate Refuge Uses (603 FW1)
This policy (603 FW 1), published in July 2006, provides a national framework for determining appropriate refuge uses. Serving as a "prescreening" for proposed uses of a national wildlife refuge prior to a compatibility determination (see below); this policy requires – for most uses - a written finding of appropriateness by the refuge manager based on 11 criteria. Findings of appropriateness require concurrence by the State for refuges located within state boundaries. These criteria include:
  - Promotes safety of participants, other visitors, and facilities.
  - Promotes compliance with applicable laws, regulations, and responsible behavior.
  - Minimizes or eliminates conflicts with fish and wildlife populations or habitat goals or objectives in a plan approved after 1997.
  - Minimizes or eliminates conflicts with other compatible wildlife-dependent recreation.
  - Minimizes conflicts with neighboring landowners.
  - Promotes accessibility and availability to a broad spectrum of the American people.
  - Promotes resource stewardship and conservation.
  - Promotes public understanding and increases public appreciation of America's natural resources and our role in managing and protecting these resources.
  - Provides reliable/reasonable opportunities to experience wildlife.
  - Uses facilities that are accessible and blend into the natural setting.
  - Uses visitor satisfaction to help define and evaluate programs.

Compatibility (603 FW2)
Lands within the System are different from other, multiple-use public lands in that, with few exceptions, they are closed to all public access and use unless specifically and legally opened (603 FW 2). No refuge use may be allowed unless it is determined to be compatible. A

compatible use is one that, in the sound professional judgment of the refuge manager, would not materially interfere with or detract from the fulfillment of the mission of the Service or the purpose of the refuge. The NWRS Administration Act identifies six wildlife-dependent recreational uses: hunting, fishing, wildlife observation, photography, environmental education, and interpretation. When compatible, these six uses become priority uses of the System. As priority public uses, they receive special consideration over other general public uses in refuge planning and management.

<u>Biological Integrity, Diversity, and Environmental Health (601 FW3)</u>
The NWRS Administration Act directs the Service to "ensure that the biological integrity, diversity, and environmental health of the System are maintained for the benefit of present and future generations of Americans…" This policy (601 FW 3) is an additional directive for refuge managers to follow while achieving refuge purpose(s) and System mission. It provides for the consideration and protection of the broad spectrum of fish, wildlife, plants, and their habitat resources found on refuges and associated ecosystems. When evaluating the appropriate management direction for refuges, refuge managers would use sound professional judgment to determine their refuges' contribution to maintenance and, where possible, restoration of biological integrity, diversity, and environmental health (BIDEH) at multiple landscape scales. Sound professional judgment incorporates field experience, knowledge of refuge resources, refuge functions within an ecosystem, applicable laws, and best available science, including consultation with others both inside and outside the Service.

<u>Wilderness (602 FW 3)</u>
Service planning policy (602 FW 3) requires the conduct of a wilderness review in association with the development of a refuge CCP. The wilderness review process has three phases: inventory, study, and recommendation. After first identifying lands and waters that meet the minimum criteria for wilderness during the inventory phase, the resulting wilderness study areas are further evaluated to determine if they merit recommendation from the Service to the Secretary of the Interior (Secretary) for inclusion in the National Wilderness Preservation System. A more complete discussion of wilderness inventory, study, and recommendation is included in Appendix F.

<u>General Guidelines for Wildlife-Dependent Recreation (605 FW1)</u>
This set of policies (605 FW 1-7), published in July 2006, defines the System's wildlife-dependent recreation policy, provides guidelines used to manage wildlife-dependent recreation on refuge lands and identifies visitor service standards.

1.4.3 National Wildlife Refuges in the Pacific

Nineteen individual NWRs are scattered across the central and western Pacific Ocean, with several refuges located on the main Hawaiian Islands and others found from Guam to American Samoa (Figure 1.1). The Hawaiian and Pacific Islands NWR Complex office, which provides administrative guidance and oversight for these 19 refuges, is located in Honolulu, Hawaii. This Complex also co-manages the newly established Papahānaumokuākea Marine National Monument along with the National Oceanic and Atmospheric Administration and the State of Hawaii.

Within this administrative structure is a subset of seven refuges known as the Remotes Complex. The Remotes Complex straddles the Equator near the center of the Pacific Ocean. They are farther from human population centers than any other U.S. area and represent one of the last frontiers and havens for fish and wildlife in the World. These remote refuges are the most widespread collection of coral reef and seabird/shorebird protected areas on the planet under a single country's jurisdiction. Only one of these seven refuges, Palmyra Atoll NWR has on-island dedicated staff members. Remotes Complex staff, located within the complex office in Honolulu, manage all the remaining refuges, including Jarvis. Staff, funding, and logistical support are often shared among these remote refuges to help defray operational costs.

The preferred alternative for the Jarvis CCP identifies several management strategies that are dependent upon activities and staff support from the Remotes Complex office, ship transportation support from other Federal agencies, or the establishment of partnerships with other organizations. Because of the great distances involved in traveling to these remote refuges, most management activities, including the simple act of visiting a refuge, are sometimes planned to occur concurrently during the same voyage. For this reason, cost estimates for management activities at Jarvis are pro-rated amongst the seven Remotes Complex refuges in the analysis of the alternatives.

Figure 1.1 Map of National Wildlife Refuges in the Pacific.

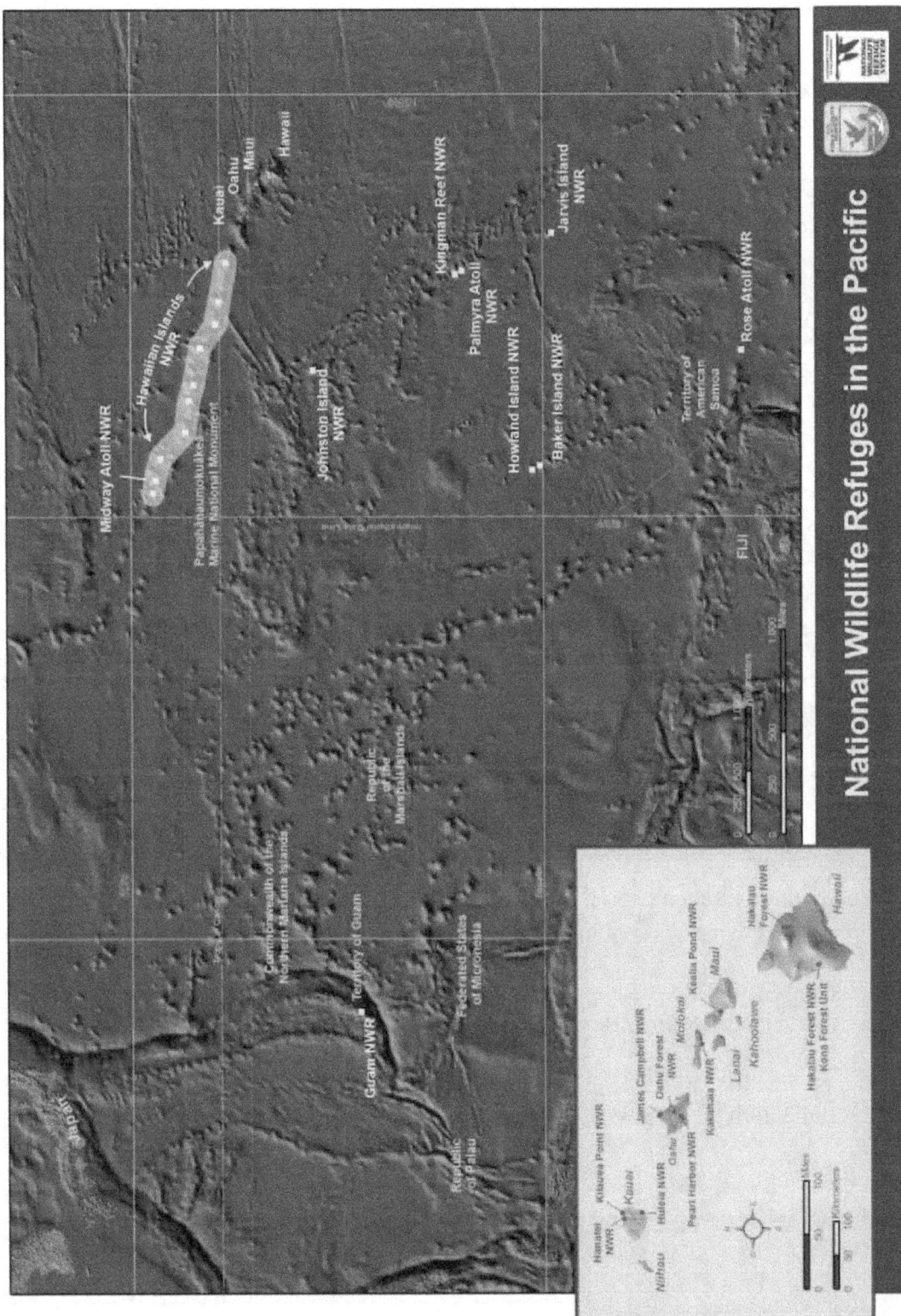

1.4.4 Refuge Establishment, Purpose, and Boundary

Refuge Establishment
Prior to refuge establishment, President Franklin D. Roosevelt signed Executive Order 7368 on May 13, 1936, placing control and jurisdiction of Jarvis Island with the Secretary of the Interior. Originally administered by the Office of Territorial Affairs, the Secretary of the Interior (Secretary), on June 27, 1974, designated Jarvis Island and its territorial sea extending to the 3 nautical mile (nmi) limit as a unit of the System (39 FR 27930).

Refuge Purpose
Refuge purposes are often times are based upon land acquisition documents and authorities. These statements give indications for the biological reason or justification for the acquisition or land transfer. Purposes listed in acquisition authorities, or legislative acts, are often general in scope. For Jarvis, this general purpose is:

"... for the development, advancement, management, conservation, and protection of fish and wildlife resources ..." (16 U.S.C. 742f (a) (4)), and ""... for the benefit of the United States Fish and Wildlife Service, in performing its activities and services. Such acceptance may be subject to the terms of any restrictive or affirmative covenant, or condition of servitude ..." (16 U.S.C. 742f (b) (1)) (Fish and Wildlife Act of 1956).

Acquisition documents often contain more specific purpose statements. The specific purpose statement for establishment of Jarvis identified in the biological ascertainment report at the time of transfer to the Service is (USFWS 1973):

"...the preservation of the complete ecosystem, terrestrial as well as marine. Special emphasis to be given to the large seabird nesting colonies."

Refuge Boundary
Jarvis is located in the central equatorial Pacific Ocean (Figure 1.2). The boundary for Jarvis includes:

"all of said island ... together with its territorial sea extending outward to the three-mile limit." (39 Federal Register 27930).

The emergent land area for Jarvis encompasses 1,273 acres and submerged lands and waters within the three-mile limit encompass 36,214 acres for a total of 37,487 acres.

Figure 1.2 Jarvis Island National Wildlife Refuge: Geographic Location and Boundary.

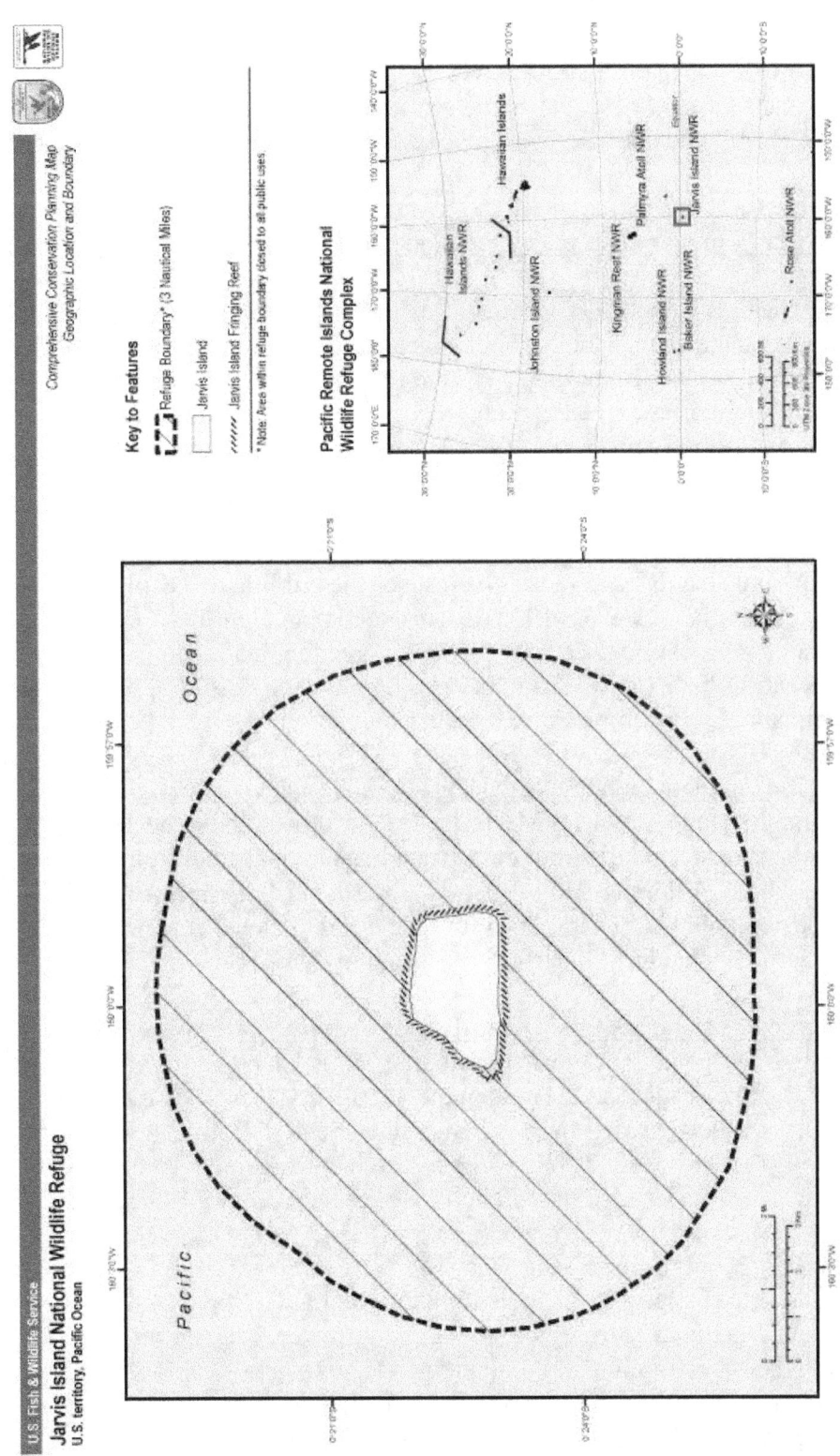

1.4.5 Regional and Ecosystem Conservation Plans

Regional and ecosystem conservation plans and initiatives are also important to evaluate and incorporate into developing each CCP. These plans typically address issues or concerns that are site specific or of regional concern, and address needs more current than when the refuge was established.

Remote Islands Ecosystem Plan: Howland Island, Baker Island, and Jarvis Island National Wildlife Refuge
The ecosystem plan for Howland, Baker, and Jarvis identifies Jarvis as "…an important site for the study of long term global climate change and periodic phenomena such as El Niño Southern Oscillation" (USFWS 1998b). The plan further describes the fringing reef as a healthy coral community resulting from its remoteness and lack of anthropogenic effects, and having 14 species of breeding seabirds and the only protected seabird island in the northern Line Islands.

Coral Reef Initiative in the Pacific: Howland Island, Baker Island, and Jarvis Island National Wildlife Refuges
The Coral Reef Initiative for Howland, Baker, and Jarvis restates the wildlife and ecological values identified in the ecosystem plan (USFWS 1998a). This document identifies three important components of the three ecosystems: "They provide a breeding platform for pelagic birds using large areas of ocean surface, offer a migratory stopover for long distance migrating shorebirds, and furnish reef habitat for shallow water organisms."

Recovery Plan for U.S. Pacific Populations of the Hawksbill Turtle (*Eretmochelys imbricate*)
Although theoretically within the range for hawksbill turtle, little is known about their biology, foraging and nesting behavior, threats, and distribution surrounding Jarvis Island. Both the National Oceanic and Atmospheric Administration – National Marine Fishery Service (NMFS) and the Service share responsibility at the Federal level for the research, management, and recovery of Pacific marine turtle populations under U.S. jurisdiction (NMFS and USFWS 1998).

Recovery Plan for U.S. Pacific Populations of the Green Turtle (*Celonia mydas*)
Few green turtles are known to forage in the waters surrounding Jarvis Island and nesting was recorded in low densities along the west coast of Jarvis in the 1930's. However, data from the area is limited and use of Jarvis may be greater than currently documented. Both the NMFS and the Service share responsibility at the Federal level for the research, management, and recovery of Pacific marine turtle populations under U.S. jurisdiction (NMFS and USFWS 1998).

U.S. Pacific Island Regional Shorebird Conservation Plan
This regional shorebird plan identifies Jarvis as being within the Central Pacific Islands Subregion. No natural wetlands are known from this subregion; however, beaches on uninhabited islands are important for shorebirds. Population and habitat goals for this subregion state that determining population size and trends for bristle-thighed curlews and other shorebirds, and their habitats is a management priority (Engilis and Naughton 2004).

United States Shorebird Conservation Plan

This nationwide shorebird plan identifies the U.S. Pacific Islands being of "critical importance for two species of Holartic breeders, bristle-thighed curlew and Pacific golden-plover." Further, this plan notes that these islands provide wintering habitat essential to the maintenance of these species as well as several other migratory shorebird species (Brown et al. 2000).

Seabird Conservation Plan, Pacific Region

This plan provides an overarching review, discussion, and identification of conservation priorities for seabirds in the U.S Pacific Islands; ranks seabirds for conservation priority; and includes specific species accounts including their conservation needs (USFWS 2005).

Central Pacific World Heritage Project

The United Nations Educational, Scientific and Cultural Organization (UNESCO) organized and convened meetings in Honolulu in June 2003, and Kiritimati Atoll in October 2004, to seek input for a proposed multi-national World Heritage project now referred to as the Central Pacific World Heritage Project (CPWHP) (UNESCO World Heritage Centre, 2003; 2004). Additional meetings and evaluations in the U.S. and Republic of Kiribati resulted in a total of 29 atolls, islands, and reefs belonging to four nations (United States, Cook Islands, Republic of Kiribati, and French Polynesia) being proposed for the multi-site, multi-jurisdictional CPWHP. To date, the Service has not acted on this proposal, but intends to do so in the future.

1.5 Planning Issues, Concerns and Opportunities

Issues, concerns, and opportunities were identified through discussions with key contacts, workshop participants, core team members, other refuge staff, and through the public scoping process. The following section summarizes issues, concerns, and opportunities from all public input received throughout the planning efforts. Six issues were identified and are described below.

Issue 1: Operational Limitations

Jarvis is located approximately 1,263 nmi from the management staff located in Honolulu, Hawaii. On average, it takes 8 days to reach Jarvis by ship, the only method of visiting the island. The key issues and concerns affecting planning and management implementation are:
- distance from refuge headquarters;
- lack of affordable and reliable transportation;
- lack of infrastructure to support field operations;
- extreme environmental conditions; and
- safety concerns and logistical capacity to land people and equipment on-island from small boats.

Issue 2: Biological and Ecological Resources

Biological and ecological information sufficient for management or conservation purposes is lacking. Due to the infrequency and limited staff time spent on Jarvis, biological and ecological information is not of sufficient frequency to allow for a detailed assessment of resources. The collection of baseline and long-term monitoring information should be a primary concern and the focus of management objectives.

Issue 3: External Forces

The threat of the introduction of invasive species from unauthorized visits, marine debris washing ashore and onto coral reefs, and vessel groundings are beyond current management control. Distance, lack of funds and staff, and the inability to have a more consistent presence on this island opens the opportunity for invasive species introductions, limits the ability to remove marine debris, and delays in the response to vessel groundings.

Global climate change (see Chapter 3.3) may also affect refuge resources, but is beyond control of refuge management staff. It is anticipated that changes in the chemical composition of the atmosphere and oceans; surface temperatures of air, land, and sea; intensity and frequency of rainfall and storm waves; and changes in sea level would have impacts on refuge resources. However, the extent and nature of these impacts, if any, is unclear and the subject of considerable academic debate.

Issue 4: Public Use Resources

The key issues related to public use are:
- adverse ecological impacts (invasive species introductions, sewage pollution, fuel spills, trash disposal, harassment of wildlife, damage to sensitive habitats such as coral reefs);
- whether any on-site public use should be allowed;
- to what extent the use should occur; and
- how the use should be managed.

Jarvis has never been formally opened to public access and use. Administratively, public access to Jarvis is managed through use of a refuge-issued Special Use Permits (SUP). Several recreational user groups such as amateur radio operators, bird watchers, history enthusiasts, destination tourists, and commercial cruise vessels have expressed interest in visiting various remote Pacific Island refuges. However, only amateur radio operators have pursued and obtained a SUP after an initial inquiry.

Issue 5: Education and Outreach

In general, Pacific Island refuges are poorly recognized by the public and our partner agencies. There are few entrance signs, no boundary signs, and little published information in popular literature. Refuge boundaries are rarely portrayed on nautical charts and other maps.

The remote location and isolation of Jarvis and other Pacific island refuges make it difficult to conduct on-site visits for educational or interpretative purposes. Thus, most educational and interpretative opportunities are necessarily delivered remotely through various media.

In addition, general interest by the public and requests to visit remote Pacific Island refuges by a growing recreational yachting community has increased recently. This interest requires the public to be better informed regarding sensitive refuge habitats, species, and regulations.

Issue 6: Communication and Cooperation

Jarvis's remoteness compels a growing list of partners and cooperators to be kept informed of and included in planning and management activities at Jarvis. Activities that staff and partner agencies/organizations share include:

- expedition planning;
- collaborative research projects; and
- jurisdictions of trust resources.

Most access for refuge staff to Jarvis has only been possible through the cooperation and participation with partner agencies such as NOAA and the U.S. Coast Guard. Many research interests are shared between Service and NOAA scientists, and collaborative research projects have been conducted in the past. Additionally, NOAA and the Service share trust resource responsibilities for marine turtles.

1.6 Refuge Vision Statement

The refuge vision statement is a broad general statement that describes what the refuge staff perceives as Jarvis's fundamental attributes and contributions to a healthy world environment. This statement will guide management activities for the lifespan of this plan, as well into the near future. The draft vision statement for Jarvis is as follows.

> *Jarvis is one of the last places in the world where the terrestrial and marine tropical island ecosystems are still intact and relatively free of human impact, offering the opportunity to serve as a living laboratory for measuring current and future human impacts to island, coral reef, and deep marine habitats. Natural, physical and ecological processes unfold with limited human interference and support a diverse community of native marine organisms including seabirds, marine mammals, turtles, fish, plants, corals, and other invertebrates. Nesting and foraging seabirds dominate the landscape and seascape while sheer isolation and solitude help us see our place in the natural world.*

1.7 Refuge Goals

Goal statements are succinct statements of a desired future condition of refuge resources. Goals comprise the whole of a refuge's effort in pursuit of its vision and lay the foundation from which all refuge activities arise. The goals for Jarvis are as follows, and will again be presented along with objectives and strategies in Chapter 2.6.

1. Conserve, manage, and protect native terrestrial habitats that are representative of remote tropical Pacific islands, primarily for the benefit of seabirds.

2. Conserve, manage, and protect native marine communities that are representative of remote tropical Pacific Islands.
3. Contribute to the recovery, protection, and management efforts for all native species with special consideration for seabirds, migratory shorebirds, Federally listed threatened and endangered species, and species of management concern.
4. Protect, maintain, enhance, and preserve the wilderness character of Jarvis's terrestrial and marine communities.
5. Jarvis's cultural and historic resources are preserved.
6. An informed, interested, and educated public appreciates remote Pacific Island NWRs wilderness values, cultural and historical resources, and their ecosystems, with special emphasis on seabirds.

Chapter 2: Alternatives, Objectives, and Strategies

2.1 Introduction to the Alternatives

This chapter describes the process used to develop alternatives, including a no-action alternative that describes the current condition and three action alternatives that describe various proposed changes to current management programs. A preferred alternative is identified; however, the preferred alternative may be modified between the draft and final documents depending upon comments received from the public or other agencies and organizations. Similarities and differences among the alternatives are presented, as are detailed descriptions of each alternative. Summary tables comparing all alternatives are also included. Goals, objectives, strategies, and the rationale for these are presented following the description of alternatives.

2.1.1 Development of Alternatives

Comments received on the preliminary set of alternatives and throughout the public scoping process ultimately resulted in the four draft management alternatives presented in this draft CCP/EA. These include a "no action" alternative (as required under NEPA) and three "action" alternatives, each of which describes strategies for managing Jarvis over the 15-year life time of the plan that might ultimately improve future conditions at the refuge. Each alternative describes a combination of wildlife and habitat management strategies designed to achieve the refuge goals and objectives. These alternatives provide different ways to address and respond to major issues, management concerns, and opportunities identified during the planning process. All of the major issues, activities, and management concerns were evaluated and addressed for each alternative. The four alternatives are summarized below:

- Alternative A - No Action. This alternative assumes no change from current management programs and is considered the baseline from which to compare the other alternatives. Specifically, the refuge would remain closed to public access, with compatible activities being allowed and administered through the refuge's Special Use Permit process. Wildlife and habitat management activities such as monitoring seabird populations, documenting the presence of invasive plant species, stockpiling marine and other debris, and using solar powered electronic radio calls to attract nesting seabirds would be restricted to the 1 to 2 day period that occur once every 2 years. Transportation to and from Jarvis would be provided by NOAA or other partners, at the discretion and capability of the partner.

- Alternative B – Preferred Alternative. This alternative describes an increase in the frequency of staff visits from once every two years to once every year. Overall, wildlife and habitat management activities would be identical as those described in the No Action alternative. The use of solar powered electronic radio calls used to encourage seabird nesting activity would be continued. Increased monitoring in the marine environment would be dependent upon partnership opportunities developed with NOAA, University of Hawaii, or other partners. Transportation to and from the island would rely upon NOAA, or other partners providing arrangements similar to those provided in the No Action

Alternative. Public use and access would remain closed and be administered as described in the No Action alternative.

- Alternative C. This alternative describes an increase in the frequency and duration of staff visits, and increases the scale and scope of management activities conducted during those visits. Concurrently staffed seasonal field camps (approximately 4 months duration) would be established on Jarvis and two other nearby refuges. Increased monitoring of seabird populations would create greater understanding of migration and nesting chronologies of various seabird species. Seasonal field camps would allow adequate time to control invasive species, and provide basic maintenance of cultural and historical resources. Removal of marine debris from the island to protect seabirds and turtles from entanglement would also occur. Transportation to and from seasonal field camps would be provided by contract vessel. Public use and access would remain closed and be administered as described in the No Action alternative.

- Alternative D. Management activities under this alternative are similar to those described in Alternative C. However, a greater level of detail and understanding of Jarvis's wildlife resources would be possible. The primary differences between these two alternatives is that a single field camp would be established on only 1 mid-Pacific island refuge in a given year. Field camps would be rotated annually between these island refuges, and transportation would be provided by a FWS-owned vessel. Public use and access would remain closed and be administered as described in the No Action alternative.

These four alternatives are described in more detail below starting with the similarities among the alternatives, followed by a detailed description of each alternative, and finally a summary that defines the rationale for selecting the Preferred Alternative.

2.2 Similarities among Alternatives

Although the alternatives differ in several ways, there are similarities (i.e. shared features or management components) among them as well. Following is a description of the features common to all the alternatives (A-D); and features common to all action alternatives (B-D).

2.2.1 Features Common to All Alternatives (A-D)

All alternatives contain some common features. These are presented below to reduce the length and redundancy of the individual alternative descriptions.

- *Baseline Monitoring of Wildlife Populations and Habitats.* At a minimum, staff visits to Jarvis requires baseline monitoring efforts to document species presence or absence, abundance, habitat condition, presence of invasive species and various other physical variables such as temperature, precipitation, wind, etc. This basic biophysical monitoring would be constant throughout the alternatives. However, some alternatives would build upon this minimum level of visitation and monitoring.

- *Voyage Preparation.* The logistics of providing adequate field camp supplies such as water, food, first aid, and communications would also remain constant. However, some alternatives would require an additional volume or frequency of subsistence supplies to support greater numbers or staff-days on the refuge.

- *Use of extraneous unnatural lighting.* Nighttime operations of the support vessel and the use of light sources by staff in the camp would be carried out in order to minimize collision and disorientation of wildlife that can be caused by light hazards. This would include minimizing lighting on the vessel and in camp, shading windows, and limiting use of hand-held lights.

- *Use of stringent quarantine protocols and when invasive species are discovered, use of IPM to eradicate or control them.* Visitors to Jarvis would be required to wear new and frozen clothing and other soft gear as outlined in quarantine protocols (Appendix D). Other quarantine precautions include prohibiting fresh fruits or vegetables, cardboard boxes, and disinfecting surfaces of tools and other hard surfaces. Time permitting; the hand pulling of weeds would occur. The selective hand spray application of herbicides or pesticides, where appropriate, may also occur.

- *Scientific Information Exchange.* Refuge staff currently attend various professional meetings and conferences related to Pacific Island and marine resources. Additionally, a minimal amount of staff time is devoted to the development of peer-reviewed journal articles and contributing to NOAA and Service sponsored Web sites. These activities would remain constant, although there may be opportunities to increase this involvement with some alternatives.

- *Preservation of Wilderness Values.* Since its establishment, Jarvis has been managed to preserve its wilderness values and characteristics even though it has never been proposed for wilderness designation. These values are intrinsic at this remote, uninhabited island and coral reef ecosystem. Management activities across all alternatives would not impinge on these values.

- *Public Access.* Since establishment, Jarvis has never been formally opened to public access and use. Access and public use remains closed across all alternatives. All individual opportunities for compatible use such as specific research projects would continue to be administered using individual SUPs.

- *Interpretation, Education, and Outreach.* Current opportunities for off-site education exist at the Maritime Museum, Honolulu, Hawaii. A hands-on exhibit representing a Pacific Island refuge is maintained to educate school-aged students about seabirds, invasive species, marine debris, and the System. Interpretative displays are also used periodically at conventions and professional meetings.

- *Protection and Preservation of Cultural Resources.* Cultural resources remain intact and in situ across all alternatives. Field camps would be situated to avoid impacts to cultural resource sites. Archaeological reconnaissance and possible testing to avoid impacts to cultural resources would be required prior to management activity that would potentially disturb surface or subsurface resources.

- *Waste Disposal at Sea.* Disposal of waste in refuge waters is prohibited under all alternatives.

- *Waste Disposal on Island.* All waste from food products, equipment, and containers that is brought onto the island will be removed during demobilization. Depending upon the duration of the site visit, human excrement will be either bagged, stored in a chemical toilet, or decomposed using portable biodegradable toilets, all of which will subsequently be removed during field camp demobilization.

- *Refuge Boundary*. There are no changes being proposed to the refuge boundary under any alternative.
- *Seabird Nesting Restoration.* All alternatives include the deployment of electronic calls as seabird nesting attraction devices designed to attract Phoenix petrels (*Pterodroma alba*) and Polynesian storm-petrels (*Nesofregetta fuliginosa*). These electronic call devices consist of solar powered speakers broadcasting calls of both species in suitable areas of the island. Both of these small ground-nesting Procellariforms are severely depleted or extirpated throughout much of their range. The mammal-free status of Jarvis Island makes it an ideal site within the species' original range to restore a breeding population of each species.

2.2.2 Features Common to All Action Alternatives (B-D)

These features are common to Alternatives B, C, and D but would not be implemented as part of the No-Action Alternative.

- *Cultural Resources Inventory.* Jarvis would be re-evaluated for the presence and condition of cultural resources. Visits that are more frequent would provide the opportunity for on-site review and documentation of cultural resources. However, the duration of the site visit across the alternatives would determine the level of review.
- *Wilderness Study Area.* A recommendation for Wilderness Study Area designation would apply to all action alternatives. However, wilderness recommendation would be postponed until an LEIS and wilderness proposal are developed for all other remote Pacific Island NWRs as part of their CCP processes.
- *Marine ecosystem monitoring.* Funding will be sought for additional exploration of deep slope resources. Use of a University of Hawaii ship equipped with a remotely operated vehicle (ROV) to operate at depths between 150 to 3,300 feet may be possible across all action alternatives.

2.3 Detailed Description of the Alternatives

A narrative description outlining each alternative follows. Additionally, Table 2.1 contrasts how various themes/issues identified in this CCP are addressed by the alternatives. Table 2.2 compares the cost estimates for each alternative.

2.3.1 Alternative A – No Action (Current Management)

This alternative assumes no change from present management programs and is considered the base from which to compare the action alternatives (Table 2-1). The Service's Remotes Complex office would continue to maintain jurisdiction and management of Jarvis Island and the associated coral reefs and marine habitats out to three nmi as a NWR. Site visits to Jarvis would occur approximately once every 2 years as they have for the past 6 years. Staff visits would be arranged through the cooperation of partner agencies such as NOAA, U.S. Coast Guard, and other organizations providing berths for refuge staff. During these staff visits, two refuge staff would spend approximately 1 to 2 days on the island conducting baseline scientific data collection, inspecting boundary signs, inventorying for the presence of invasive species, visiting cultural resources, and collecting and stockpiling marine debris. The brief and infrequent visits in this alternative preclude any habitat management other than stockpiling entrapment hazards that may wash ashore or remain because of human habitation during the guano mining and military eras.

Marine vessels capable of traveling the open ocean for extended periods are the only opportunity for transportation to Jarvis. In the recent years, NOAA, the U.S. Coast Guard, and private charter vessels have all provided transportation. Typically, Baker, Howland, and Johnston Island NWR (Johnston) are visited as part of the first leg of a comprehensive biennial NOAA scientific ship expedition to all central Pacific Ocean insular properties. For this first leg, the ship arrives at Johnston after 3 days of travel from Honolulu. Four days of research time are spent at Johnston before departing for Howland. After 7 days of travel, the ship arrives at Howland and spends the next 4 days at both Howland and nearby Baker conducting research before departing for American Samoa. Jarvis is typically completed on the second leg of the expedition. Biologists are not allowed to go ashore if surf conditions are too rough near Howland, Baker, or Jarvis. Consequently, only marine surveys would be conducted. Based upon prior attempts, there is a 50% chance that biologists will make it onto Howland, Baker, or Jarvis. After 5 additional days of travel, the ship arrives at Pago Pago, American Samoa, allowing a change-out of crew and scientists for the second leg of the expedition, continuing from American Samoa to Rose Atoll NWR, Jarvis, Palmyra Atoll NWR, and Kingman Reef NWR. An equal amount of time, about 25 days, is spent for the second leg of the expedition to conduct research and return to Honolulu

Once on-site on Jarvis, if wind and wave conditions warrant the launch of a landing vessel (typically a small outboard type inflatable boat), the marine vessel will anchor or remain stationary during the deployment of the field camp, only venturing away from the island to complete marine surveys. The field camp itself generally consists of two individuals, typically biologists to carry out biological surveys and other duties, and camping gear consisting of tents, sleeping equipment, food, water, and needed survey equipment. Cooking gear is rarely deployed since staff are only on-island for 1 to 2 days with most of that time being engaged in work activities.

While on-island, the biologists will document all bird species present, count individuals, determine if any and the extent of nesting, casually observe vegetation and record species presence or absence, or the presence of any invasive species. Cultural sites will be visited with observations made about condition and deterioration. The only active management that occurs during these site visits is the collection and on-island stockpile of marine debris that washes ashore and poses a threat to seabirds and other wildlife that utilize Jarvis. Any evidence of illegal activity such as unauthorized access will also be documented. Photographs will record general habitat conditions; however, further habitat assessments would not occur. Although no specific activities occur with respect to wilderness values, the simple fact that a 1 to 2 day field camp consisting of temporary lodging arrangements and minimal activity is consistent with maintaining the wilderness values of the area.

During the period that the biologists are on Jarvis, marine scientists from NOAA, the Service, and other partner organizations such as the University of Hawaii conduct surveys and monitoring activities of the marine environment. Some monitoring activities occur on-board the vessel, while others require the use of SCUBA equipment and divers. All of the marine scientists, however, are based on the vessel awaiting the conclusion of terrestrial surveys and thus do not come ashore. Marine scientists typically collect information on currents, weather, temperature, chemical composition of the water, and the abundance and distribution of coral and fish species. Specific marine-based surveys known as Rapid Ecological Assessments (REA) are conducted and ecological data such as fish species, abundance, and predator prey relationships is collected. Data is also collected from permanently marked coral transects which document coral species, age class, and percent coral cover. These data are collected over a 2-day period (six 1-hour dives). Following the voyage, data is provided to the Service that includes a full range of oceanographic, bathymetric, and marine biological data. Once field operations are complete, or the weather becomes increasingly inclement, the field camp is demobilized and all equipment and personnel are transported back to the research vessel. A NOAA cruise report for the first leg is completed before the ship arrives at Pago Pago. Service trip reports are completed, distributed, and filed once field staff returns to the Honolulu office.

2.3.2 Alternative B - (Preferred Alternative)

Management under Alternative B would increase the frequency of staff visits to Jarvis and would not alter the current management regime. Habitat assessments and wildlife monitoring data would continue to be collected as described in the No Action Alternative. The travel to, establishment of, and conduct of field camps would also remain the same. The primary difference between Alternative A and Alternative B is the frequency of visitation from once every two years to once every year respectively. Thus, at the end of the 15-year lifespan of the plan, it is anticipated that there will have been 15 visits to Jarvis. In order to meet the increase in the number of site visits, refuge staff in Honolulu would be administratively burdened to seek additional funding sources and develop partnerships for additional visits. This may take the form of producing internal project proposals (RONS), or seeking funding support through grants or partnerships with other agencies, research institutions, and non-government organizations. The scale and scope of marine surveys would also be maintained. At a minimum, marine scientists would resurvey REAs and other transects described in Alternative A.

2.3.3 Alternative C

Management activity on Jarvis would increase under this alternative. Seasonal field camps lasting approximately 4 months would be established concurrently on Jarvis and two other remote Pacific Ocean refuges (Howland and Baker). Subsequent years would find the seasonal field camps deployed during alternating 4 month periods. Thus, the field camp would return to Jarvis once every year during a different 4 month period. At the end of three years, it is expected that field camp staff would have spent twelve months on the island and have been present on the island during each month of the year. Due to the relatively short duration of each field camp, it would be possible to deploy and demobilize without any re-supply trips. Thus, a contract vessel for two charter periods (deployment and demobilization) would be required. Yearly funding to charter a research vessel would be required to implement this alternative. Aside from deployment and demobilization, no small vessels would be required during field camp operations.

Access provided by a charter vessel would substantially increase Service presence and ability to monitor, survey, restore, and otherwise manage refuge resources. Seabird species nesting at latitudes near the equator are extremely asynchronous and vary between years in their schedule of breeding. Longer periods of residency at Jarvis would foster a better understanding of breeding chronology of seabirds. Longer visits would enable the staff to map vegetation and detect rare species of all taxa that may be missed on shorter trips. Surveys of shorebirds and terrestrial invertebrates would also be conducted. By concurrently operating field camps on these three refuges it would be possible to compare, wildlife use between the refuges, but it would not be able to provide a complete assessment of annual use on any one individual refuge. Nearshore surveys of the marine environment, not requiring SCUBA could be increased, but due to safety concerns, most marine surveys would only occur during the period when the transport vessel was near the island during deployment and demobilization.

Terrestrial and marine invasive plant and invertebrate species have the capacity to alter plant and animal communities, specifically posing a threat to seabird nesting habitat and coral reefs. Staff being present on the island each year would provide the opportunity to complete comprehensive surveys for both native and exotic species. The extended duration of site visits will allow for the early detection of any exotic or invasive species, and provide for the rapid response and control before any invasive species has the ability to negatively affect refuge resources. Invasive species control would be in the form of hand-pulling plants and algae, hand spray applications of herbicide or insecticide or physical removal of invertebrates such as crown-of-thorns starfish. It should be noted again, however, that concerns for ocean safety during extended field camps without nearby vessel support will severely limit marine surveys and activities.

Marine debris poses an entanglement threat to seabirds and turtles. The extended field camp operations proposed in Alternative C would provide refuge staff the opportunity to not only collect and stockpile marine debris such as discarded fishing nets and plastic waste, but prepare the debris for off-site removal during demobilization activities.

Additional time on the island would allow field camp staff to conduct visual surveys for sea turtle use of nearshore waters. Turtles are often found basking on shorelines, or foraging in shallow nearshore waters where they find plant growth to graze. Habitat use and behaviors of turtles found in the area would be documented in this alternative. While surveys could be conducted to document turtle use in the nearshore waters, the availability of a contract vessel only during deployment and demobilization would limit the ability to search for other sites of turtle or marine mammal use outside of nearshore waters.

Remotely operated cameras, hydrophones, listening devices, and satellite linkages may also be used to collect data and imagery primarily on seabird use, breeding chronology, habitat selection, seabird productivity, and other ecological attributes. These biotic and abiotic characteristics could be monitored during periods when field camps are not present on the island. These data would also be used for law enforcement purposes to detect trespass and for monitoring condition of vegetation, presence or absence of all avian species using the refuge, monitoring of invertebrate (land crab) population indices, and to detect invasive species. However, the level of implementation and the use of this technology would be dependent upon available funding.

A limited amount of time would be available for the maintenance of existing cultural and historical resources. For instance, it would be reasonable to assume that minor masonry repair or repainting of the Jarvis Light day beacon could be accomplished during one of the 3-year periods. Cultural resource surveys would need to be completed prior to any cultural resource restoration and maintenance, or the establishment of the field camp.

Additional research opportunities would present themselves with a 4 month field camp. The primary increase would be in documenting the effects of a changing global environment. While it is certain that our climate is changing, it is uncertain how this change will affect mid-Pacific Ocean islands and their wildlife resources. Changes in sea level, current patterns, temperature, nutrients, and storm intensities could all have impacts on these areas, or the distribution of seabird food resources. Without the opportunity to monitor these parameters, it will be impossible to discuss their impacts, and ultimately to make any changes to management activities to minimize the impacts.

A regularly chartered vessel would also provide the opportunity to provide a law enforcement presence, better understand the equatorial Pacific Island ecosystems, and increase opportunities for cooperation with partner institutions, organizations and agencies. A chartered vessel would allow refuge staff be more time efficient and independent of schedules and availability of other agencies and organizations for access to Jarvis and other refuges.

2.3.4 Alternative D

Alternative D proposes to establish a year-round field camp on Jarvis, with provisions to rotate the camp to Howland, Baker, Johnston Island NWR and Rose Atoll NWR in subsequent and alternating years. The purchase of a Service vessel for field camp safety and support, and to increase the ability to monitor and manage refuge resources of all remote Pacific Island refuges is an integral component of this alternative. Interim staff change and re-supply trips for a 12 month field camp would occur a minimum of three times per year. A Service-owned vessel could also be stationed and available on-site to complete additional surveys, especially of the marine system.

All wildlife populations, particularly seabirds, could be monitored in greater detail. Annual nesting chronology, seabird recruitment by species, nest site selection, and other biological and ecological parameters could be documented. Any invasive species that are detected could be controlled and eradicated in the same manner as described in Alternative C. A rotation among Pacific Island refuges, also including Johnston Island, and Rose Atoll NWRs, would allow each island to host an annual field camp once every 5 years. Coordination with other agencies sponsoring vessel access and affording berths for Service personnel would continue under this alternative, including possible re-supply and staff change-outs. In addition, the Service would also be able to provide access to Jarvis and other refuges for visiting researchers, archeologists, and cultural resource specialists. The use and benefit of remotely operated cameras, hydrophones, listening devices, and satellite linkages are identical to those described in Alternative C.

Surveys and monitoring efforts under this alternative would provide the greatest understanding and most biologically effective management of refuge resources. Research and documentation beyond basic qualitative surveys and monitoring would be encouraged and enhanced, with the opportunity for Jarvis and other Pacific Island refuges to serve as baseline sites for monitoring global climate change and locations where seabird foraging ecology as it relates to changing oceanographic conditions near the equator could be investigated.

2.3.5 Summary

The ability of the No Action and Preferred Alternatives to contribute to meeting the mission of the System, "...to administer a national network of lands and waters for the conservation, management, and where appropriate, restoration of the fish, wildlife, and plant resources and their habitats within the United States for the benefit of present and future generations of Americans." is limited. Likewise, the No Action and the Preferred Action provide a minimal benefit to meeting the refuge purpose of, "...the preservation of the complete ecosystem, terrestrial as well as marine. Special emphasis to be given to large seabird nesting seabird colonies." A 1 to 2 day visit to the island once every 2 years or once every year respectively does not provide the opportunity for refuge staff to complete anything other than basic biological surveys of species presence or absence. Restoration, preservation, or protection of terrestrial and marine ecosystems, or nesting seabirds is not possible with the No Action or Preferred Alternative.

Alternative C and Alternative D both contribute to meeting the refuge purpose and System mission by providing the opportunity to actively work toward restoration of nesting seabird populations, potentially controlling invasive species (early detection, rapid response), removing marine debris harmful to individual animals, and contributing to our general understanding of the implications and impacts of global climate change on seabird populations.

However, lack of projected budget and staffing preclude management staff from looking for increased management activity beyond Alternative B. It is for this reason that Alternative B has been selected as the Preferred Alternative. If, during the lifetime of this plan, budget and staffing become available to pursue Alternative C or D, then the CCP will be reevaluated with the potential selection of a new Preferred Alternative. Until that time, the Service is proposing Alternative B as the Preferred Alternative.

2.4 Alternatives Considered but Eliminated from Detailed Study

The concept of placing Jarvis in custodial status, or in other words doing less than the No Action alternative was considered but eliminated from further study. At present, refuge staff visits Jarvis once every two years, thereby managing the refuge just above a custodial or bare minimum level. Reducing the frequency of current staff visitation would not be sufficient to meet the purposes for which the refuge was established, or the obligations of several laws such as the Migratory Bird Treaty Act, Endangered Species Act, or the Administration Act. Custodial status for Jarvis – not visiting or preparing to visit - would reduce or eliminate any management activity to meet these obligations. In addition, the current limited visitation to the island ensures U.S. sovereignty. Eliminating visitation by placing the refuge in custodial status may jeopardize the U.S. claim of territorial ownership. Thus, custodial status as an alternative was not further evaluated.

Two Wilderness Study Areas were evaluated and determined to meet the minimum criteria for wilderness recommendation. Recommendation for wilderness designation as a component of any alternative was not considered at this time, but will be included in a LEIS at the completion of the CCP process for all other remote Pacific island refuges.

No other alternatives or components of alternatives were considered beyond those mentioned above.

Table 2.1 Summary of CCP Actions, by Alternative

Key Themes/Issues	Alternative A No Action (Current Management)	Alternative B Preferred Alternative	Alternative C	Alternative D
		Access to Refuge		
Voyage Preparation and Administration	Logistic planning required for 1 to 2 day visit and a 20-26 day voyage. Funding required for passenger aboard partner vessel, one trip every 2 years.	Logistic planning required for 1 to 2 day visit and a 20-26 day voyage. Funding required for passenger aboard partner or charter vessel, one trip every year.	Logistic planning required for 4 month long field camp. Funding required for two contract vessel trips per year, but is cost-shared with other NWRs.	Logistic planning for year long field camp. Funding required annually for vessel operation, but is cost-shared with other NWRs.
Method/Cost of Voyage Transportation	Transportation provided aboard partner vessels. No transportation cost to FWS incurred. Least expensive of all alternatives.	Transportation provided aboard partner vessels with additional effort to charter and partner. No cost on partner vessel. Charter vessel would incur cost of one charter per year. Least expensive of all action alternatives.	Transportation provided aboard partner vessels on irregular basis. Chartered vessel required on regular basis would incur cost of two charters per year, pro-rated among 3 refuges. Most expensive of all alternatives.	Transportation provided aboard partner vessels. Service-owned vessel required would incur annual cost, with cost pro-rated among 7 refuges. Slightly less than most expensive alternative.
Frequency of Site Visit	One- to 2- day visit every 2 years.	One- to 2-day visit every year.	Annually host a 4-month per year field camp.	A 12-month long field camp hosted every 5 years.

Key Themes/Issues	Alternative A No Action (Current Management)	Alternative B Preferred Alternative	Alternative C	Alternative D
Field Camp Duration and Staff Required	One- to 2- persons overnight for 1 to 2 days.	One- to 2-persons overnight for 1 to 2 days.	Two- to 3- person seasonal field camp established concurrently on Howland and two other nearby refuge islands.	Two- to 3- person year-round field camp established on Howland and rotated annually with nearby refuge islands.
Quarantine Procedures	Standard, strict visitation and importation restrictions are in place across all alternatives to control threat for invasive species.	Same as Alternative A.	Same as Alternative A.	Same as Alternative A.
Seabirds, Other Wildlife, and Habitats				
Seabird Monitoring	Basic monitoring of seabird species, abundance, and nesting status occurs every other year with a 1- to 2- day monitoring period.	Basic monitoring of seabird species, abundance, and nesting status occurs once every year with a 1- to 2- day monitoring period.	Fundamental monitoring of nesting chronology, seasonality as well as species presence and abundance occurs once every 8 months with up to a 4 months duration monitoring period.	Fundamental monitoring of nesting chronology, seasonality as well as species presence and abundance occurs once every 5 years with a 12-month duration monitoring period.

Key Themes/Issues	Alternative A No Action (Current Management)	Alternative B Preferred Alternative	Alternative C	Alternative D
Seabird Nesting Restoration	Seabird nest attraction devices (electronic bird calls) currently on-island, but inoperative. Maintenance of equipment occurs every other year. Monitoring for seabird response occurs once every other year with a 1- to 2-day monitoring period.	Seabird nest attraction devices (electronic bird calls) placed on-island. Maintenance of equipment occurs annually. Monitoring for seabird response occurs once every year with a 1- to 2-day monitoring period.	Use of remote cameras, in addition to electronic calls increases monitoring activity. Maintenance of equipment occurs annually. Monitoring for seabird response occurs once every 8-months during a 4-month monitoring period. Remote cameras allow continuous monitoring.	Use of remote cameras, in addition to electronic calls increases monitoring activity. Maintenance of equipment occurs annually. Monitoring for seabird response occurs once every 5 years during a 12-month monitoring period. Remote cameras allow continuous monitoring.
Other Wildlife and Habitat Monitoring	Each visit will document species presence or absence of species, presence of invasive species, and abiotic variables (temperature, wind speed, etc…).	Each visit will document species presence or absence of species, presence of invasive species, and abiotic variables (temperature, wind speed, etc…).	Each visit will document species presence or absence, abundance, habitat condition, presence and distribution of invasive species, and abiotic variables (temperature, wind speed, etc…).	Each visit will document species presence or absence, abundance, habitat condition, presence and distribution of invasive species, and abiotic variables (temperature, wind speed, etc…).
Vegetation Mapping	None.	None.	Mapping of vegetation will occur seasonally during field camps, but will only be capable of documenting seasonal growth patterns.	Mapping of vegetation will occur during field camps. Annual growth patterns documented, but not repeated for 5 years.

Key Themes/Issues	Alternative A No Action (Current Management)	Alternative B Preferred Alternative	Alternative C	Alternative D
Habitat Management Activities	No habitat management activities occur other than collection and stockpile of marine and other debris.	No habitat management activities occur other than collection and stockpile of marine and other debris.	Control of invasive species occurs as occurrences are detected.	Control of invasive species occurs as occurrences are detected.
Wilderness				
Wilderness Resource Management	Refuge activities will continue to preserve wilderness resource values.	Management activities will continue to preserve wilderness resource values.	Management activities will continue to preserve wilderness resource values.	Management activities will continue to preserve wilderness resource values.
Wilderness Study Area	No current WSA.	WSA identified. Wilderness recommendation delayed until all Pacific Island CCPs are complete.	WSA identified. Wilderness recommendation delayed until all Pacific Island CCPs are complete.	WSA identified. Wilderness recommendation delayed until all Pacific Island CCPs are complete.
Marine Monitoring				
Marine Exploration	No current activity.	Deep slope monitoring by ROV proposed, but dependent upon funding.	Deep slope monitoring by ROV proposed, but dependent upon funding.	Deep slope monitoring by ROV proposed, but dependent upon funding.
Marine Monitoring	Marine ecosystem monitored. REA and established surveys completed once every two years.	Marine ecosystem monitored. REA and established surveys completed once every year. No new surveys.	Marine ecosystem monitored. REA and established surveys completed twice per year. No new surveys proposed.	Marine ecosystem monitored. REA and established surveys completed twice per year. Additional survey sites possible.

Key Themes/Issues	Alternative A No Action (Current Management)	Alternative B Preferred Alternative	Alternative C	Alternative D
Cultural Resources				
Cultural Resource	Cultural resources preserved.	Cultural resources preserved. On-site cultural resource survey if funding allows.	Cultural resources preserved. On-site cultural resource survey required prior to establishment of seasonal field camp.	Cultural resources preserved. On-site cultural resource survey required prior to establishment of year-long field camp.
Recreational, Educational and Research Use				
Recreational, Educational, and Research Use	Public access would remain closed. Proposed uses by researchers and other visitors managed by issuance of Special Use Permits on a case-by-case basis. Opportunities for environmental education exist off-site.	Same as Alternative A.	Same as Alternative A.	Same as Alternative A.

2.5 Comparison of Alternatives A-D Funding Requirements

The costs associated with implementing each Alternative are shown in Table 2-3. For Alternative A (No Action), the costs incurred by the Service are associated with staff working on the island for 1 to 2 days once every two years and relies on the ability of refuge staff to be transported on a NOAA research or partner vessel to Jarvis. The costs associated with Alternative B include staff working on the island for 1 to 2 days and relies on the ability of refuge staff to be transported on a NOAA research vessel or another vessel provided through other partnerships or grant funding to facilitate yearly staff visits. Alternative C includes costs for two vessel charters per year to deploy and demobilize a seasonal field camp (4-month deployment of 2 personnel) to survey, restore and otherwise manage refuge resources. The adjusted annual personnel and operating costs for Alternative C reflect the pro rated amount for the Jarvis portion of establishing concurrent field camps on Howland, Baker and Jarvis. Alternative D includes the cost of acquiring and maintaining a vessel to facilitate the establishment of a year-round field camp that would be deployed once every five years in a rotational schedule that would include deployments at Howland, Baker, and Jarvis as well as Johnston Atoll and Rose Atoll, in the other years. The vessel purchase and operational costs in Alternative D represents costs that are distributed among all remote island refuges that would utilize this vessel to accomplish management activities throughout these Central Pacific Ocean locations. The adjusted annual cost for Alternative D reflects the pro-rated amount it would cost to implement the alternative at Jarvis.

Table 2.2 Estimated Annual Cost Comparison of Various Field Camp Configurations.

Field Camp Budget for Jarvis	Alternative A	Alternative B	Alternative C	Alternative D
Staff	$17,000 (0.3 FTE every 2 years)	$34,000 (0.3 FTE per year)	$66,000 (0.66 FTE per year)	$200,000 (2 FTE once every 5 years)
Supplies	$5,000	$7,000	$100,000	$200,000
Remote Sensing equipment	N/A	N/A	$100,000	N/A
Remote Sensing operations	N/A	N/A	$20,000	$20,000
Deep sea exploration	N/A	$25,000 per submersible vessel dive	$25,000 per submersible vessel dive	$25,000 per submersible vessel dive
Seabird recolonization initiative	N/A	$10,000	$10,000	$10,000
Vessel Charter	N/A	N/A	$12,000/day for 50 days = $600,000 per year	N/A
Vessel Purchase (one time cost)	N/A	N/A	N/A	$ 8 million
Vessel operation	N/A	N/A	N/A	$200,000 once every 5 years
Adjusted annual personnel and operating costs	$22,000/yr	$76,000/yr	$256,000/yr	$210,000/yr

2.6 Refuge Goals, Objectives, Strategies, and Rationale

Goals and objectives are the unifying elements of successful refuge management. They identify and focus management priorities, resolve issues, and link to refuge purposes, Service policy, and the Refuge System Mission.

A CCP describes management actions that help bring a refuge closer to its vision. A vision broadly reflects the refuge purposes, the Refuge System mission and goals, other statutory requirements, and larger-scale plans as appropriate. Goals then define general targets in support of the vision, followed by objectives that direct effort into incremental and measurable steps toward achieving those goals. Finally, strategies identify specific tools and actions to accomplish objectives.

In the development of this CCP, the Service has prepared an environmental assessment. The environmental assessment evaluates alternative sets of management actions derived from a variety of management goals, objectives and implementation strategies.

The goals for Jarvis over the next fifteen years under the CCP are presented on the following pages. Each goal is followed by the objectives that pertain to that goal. The goal order does not imply any priority in this CCP. Some objectives pertain to multiple goals and have simply been placed in the most reasonable spot. Similarly, some strategies pertain to multiple objectives. Following the goals, objectives, and strategies is a brief rationale intended to provide further background information pertaining to importance of an objective relative to legal mandates for managing units of the NWRS including refuge purpose, trust resource responsibilities (federally listed Threatened and Endangered species and migratory birds), and maintaining/restoring biological integrity, diversity, and environmental health.

Readers, please note the following:

The objective statement as written is the objective statement that applies to the Service's Preferred Alternative, Alternative 2. If an objective is not in a particular alternative, a blank is used to indicate that this objective is not addressed in that alternative. Below each objective statement are the strategies that could be employed in order to accomplish the objectives. Check marks alongside each strategy show which alternatives include that strategy. If a column for a particular alternative does not include a check mark for a listed strategy, it means that strategy will not be used in that alternative.

Goal 1: Conserve, manage, and protect native terrestrial habitats that are representative of remote tropical Pacific islands, primarily for the benefit of seabirds.

Objective 1a: Conserve, manage, and protect habitat for nesting seabirds.				
Upon CCP approval and throughout the life of the CCP, conserve, manage, and protect a mosaic of approximately 1,273 acres of terrestrial habitat consisting of 73 acres of beach and beach strand, 500 acres as short grass and forbs, 200 acres as scrub shrub, and 500 acres as bare ground on Jarvis Island as nesting habitat for 11 seabird species.				
Alternatives	Alt A	Alt B	Alt C	Alt D
Objective as written above applies to Alternatives (✓)	✓	✓	✓	✓
Strategies Applied to Achieve Objective	Alt A	Alt B	Alt C	Alt D
Conduct and record incidental observations of invasive species.	✓	✓	✓	✓
Control and where possible, eradicate invasive species (e.g., crabgrass) using IPM tools including hand pulling and selective application of pesticides.			✓	✓
Eradicate mammalian pests (e.g., mice) using IPM tools as needed to protect nesting seabirds.			✓	✓

Adhere to strict quarantine protocols for all island visitors (see Appendix D).	✓	✓	✓	✓
Collect and stockpile marine and other human debris not considered to be historically important.	✓	✓	✓	✓
Remove stockpiled marine and other debris.			✓	✓

Rationale:

The 11 nesting seabird species on Jarvis utilize all island habitats (see Chapter 3.9.1 and Appendix B). Masked and brown boobies prefer to nest on bare open ground. Gray-backed, sooty, and white tern, and brown and blue grey noddy also nest on the surface, but are tolerant of vegetated areas. Lesser frigatebirds, typically known as a shrub nesting species, are found exclusively on the ground at Jarvis. Red-tailed tropicbirds prefer shaded areas and can be found nesting on the surface, under coral slabs, or in shrubs. Red-footed booby and great frigatebird are the only two exclusive shrub nesting species.

The Seabird Conservation Plan (2005) recognizes remote Pacific islands as providing important and varied breeding habitat, specifically Jarvis as being important for ground nesting species. Additionally, the plan recognizes that near-shore waters provide areas of upwelling currents with important food resources for seabirds.

Maintaining the island free of mammalian predators, invasive insects, and invasive plants is critical for seabird survival (USFWS 2005). Strict quarantine protocols have been previously established for all island visitors in order to eliminate the threat of introducing invasive plants, insects, and animals (see Appendix D).

Marine and other human generated debris poses an entanglement threat for multiple wildlife species. Stockpiling debris can reduce the overall area impacted, thereby reducing the entanglement threat.

Objective 1b: Increase baseline information on terrestrial habitat.				
Within 15 years of the CCP approval, conduct monitoring to determine vegetation species presence/absence and distribution on Jarvis Island.				
Alternatives	Alt A	Alt B	Alt C	Alt D
Objective as written above applies to Alternatives (✓)	✓	✓	✓	✓
Strategies Applied to Achieve Objective	Alt A	Alt B	Alt C	Alt D
Document presence/absence island vegetation.	✓	✓	✓	✓
Conduct inventory of plant species distribution, including use of GPS and vegetation transects.			✓	✓

Coordinate with Regional Office GIS staff to assess and/or develop remote sensing capability to map and monitor island habitats.		✓	✓	✓

Rationale:

In general, insufficient time has been spent on Jarvis to adequately quantify habitat on Jarvis, and how this habitat relates to seabird biology. Collection of baseline biological information is essential to adequately understand and manage the refuge. Although it is known that the 11 nesting seabird species use all habitats on Jarvis, this information has only been obtained from the short duration, infrequent visits (1 to 2 days every 2 years) to the island. There has been no quantitative assessment of breeding species habitat associations. The distribution and delineation of habitats itself has been estimated, but never been quantified. Remotely collected data may provide an option for data collection in the absence of being capable of visiting Jarvis.

Goal 2: Conserve, manage, and protect native marine communities that are representative of remote tropical Pacific islands.

Objective 2a: Conserve, manage, and protect marine habitat.

Upon CCP approval, conserve, manage, and protect approximately 36,214 acres of submerged lands consisting of an estimated 3,000 acres coral reef and 33,214 acres of deep water/pelagic habitat on Jarvis.

Alternatives	Alt A	Alt B	Alt C	Alt D
Objective as written above applies to Alternatives (✓)	✓	✓	✓	✓

Strategies Applied to Achieve Objective	Alt A	Alt B	Alt C	Alt D
Use IPM tools to control and where possible, eradicate invasive marine species (e.g. crown-of-thorns starfish).				✓
Collect, remove, and stockpile marine debris from shallow coral reefs.				✓
Continue and expand partnership with NOAA to manage coral reef ecosystems.	✓	✓	✓	✓

Rationale:

The conservation and protection of the Nation's coral reefs is becoming increasingly important for agencies with responsibility to manage and conserve those (Executive Orders 13089 and 13158). Because the refuge boundary for Jarvis extends to 3 nmi from the island shoreline, all coral reefs are contained within the refuge boundary. Threats to the coral reef system include invasive species such as crown-of-thorns starfish and marine debris (e.g. abandoned fishing gear) that collects on corals, smothering or breaking them. The responsibility for protecting, managing, and conserving coral reef ecosystems is shared with NOAA. The Service and NOAA often participate in joint management activities throughout the Pacific, however, no active management activities have occurred at Jarvis.

Objective 2b: Increase baseline information on marine community.				
Within 15 years of CCP approval, monitor: coral species density, diversity, and distribution; fish species presence/absence and habitat associations; sea turtle species presence/absence; and marine mammal species presence/absence.				
Alternatives	Alt A	AltB2	Alt C	Alt D
Objective as written above applies to Alternatives (✓)	✓	✓	✓	✓
Strategies Applied to Achieve Objective	Alt A	Alt B	Alt C	Alt D
Conduct and record incidental observations of corals, fish, sea turtles, marine mammals, and their habitats.	✓	✓	✓	✓
Accompany NOAA or other scientific partners on marine surveys.	✓	✓	✓	✓
Conduct REA (Rapid Ecological Assessments) on all existing survey routes to document coral, fish and turtle density, diversity, distribution, and habitat associations.	✓	✓	✓	✓
Develop proposals and conduct deep slope marine surveys by ROV (remotely operated vessel) to document presence/absence of deep slope coral and fish species .		✓	✓	✓
Conduct comprehensive survey for invasive species.				✓
Increase level of REA and other marine habitat surveys by 20%.				✓
Conduct specific surveys for marine mammal presence/absence.				✓
Rationale:				

Responsibility for managing marine resources is shared with NOAA, and has led to many cooperative studies. Unlike the logistic constraints of completing terrestrial surveys, marine surveys are conducted throughout the entire time that the marine transport vessel is at Jarvis. Additionally, since most site visits to Jarvis are aboard NOAA research vessels, the purpose of these voyages is to conduct marine surveys and studies. Consequently, a full compliment of up to 20 marine researchers and 40 support staff contribute to conducting marine surveys across all alternatives. As a result, marine surveys are more comprehensive than terrestrial surveys on Jarvis.

REAs constitute baseline monitoring of the marine ecosystem, and are one component of all alternative strategies. Further expansion of REA's could be accomplished only as a component of Alternative D.

Additional surveys (marine mammals, deep slope), as described beginning with Alternative B can be achieved as components of cooperative efforts with other agencies or research organizations. As an example, little is known of marine mammal use surrounding Jarvis, although it is known that some species are found in the vicinity.

The Marine Mammal Commission has encouraged the Service to generate partnerships with NOAA to help document baseline information. Developing additional partnerships with NOAA or other organizations may also assist in meeting terrestrial objectives by providing the opportunity for additional trips to Jarvis.

Goal 3: Contribute to the recovery, protection, and management efforts for all native species with special consideration for seabirds, migratory shorebirds, federally listed threatened and endangered species, and species of management concern.

Objective 3a: Develop baseline migratory bird and other species information.				
Within 10 years of CCP approval, conduct monitoring (in rank order) to determine: seabird species presence/absence, relative abundance, breeding chronology, distribution, and habitat use; presence/absence of shorebirds; presence/absence and distribution of sea turtles; and presence/absence of terrestrial invertebrates on Jarvis Island. The desired conditions by which this will be met is understanding of the complete annual chronology for 5 of 11 nesting seabird species; population trend data over the 10-year period for all 11 nesting seabird species; and the presence/absence and distribution of shorebirds, turtles and other terrestrial invertebrates.				
Alternatives	Alt A	Alt B	Alt C	Alt D
Objective as written above applies to Alternatives (✓)	✓	✓	✓	✓
Strategies Applied to Achieve Objective	Alt A	Alt B	Alt C	Alt D
Record incidental observations of all species presence/absence, relative abundance, and distribution.	✓	✓	✓	✓
Conduct seabird monitoring activities for breeding chronology, and habitat use.			✓	✓
Coordinate with Migratory Bird Office and Office of Refuge Biology, Region 1 Regional Office to develop specific monitoring needs and data collection protocols.			✓	✓
Rationale:				
The Seabird Conservation Plan (2005) repeatedly recognizes the importance of the U.S. Pacific Islands in providing predator-free seabird nesting and roosting environments. Their protected status, in concert with nearby marine forage resources contribute to their importance. The Seabird Plan further identifies population monitoring inventories are insufficient to accurately detect or monitor populations, suggesting instead that a rigorous collection of population data is needed. In addition to Jarvis being recognized as important habitat for seabirds, the U.S. Pacific Islands Regional Shorebird Conservation Plan (2004) lists determining baseline information for bristle-thighed curlews, and other species, as the goal of the Central				

Pacific Islands Subregion. The endangered species recovery plans for both species of sea turtles indicate that little is known about their biology in the central Pacific. Data on other terrestrial wildlife species found on Jarvis Island is lacking.

Objective 3b: Restore breeding populations for 2 seabird species.				
Within 10 years of CCP approval, establish up to 5 nesting pairs each of Phoenix petrel (*Pterodroma alba*) and Polynesian storm-petrel (*Nesofregetta fuliginosa*) during a minimum of three consecutive years on Jarvis Island.				
Alternatives	Alt A	Alt B	Alt C	Alt D
Objective as written above applies to Alternatives (✓)		✓	✓	✓
Strategies Applied to Achieve Objective	Alt A	Alt B	Alt C	Alt D
Implement and maintain electronic calling devices to promote nesting		✓	✓	✓
Coordinate with RO and develop capabilities for remote surveillance equipment			✓	✓
Rationale:				
The Seabird Conservation Plan (2005) recognizes the Polynesian storm-petrel may flourish on Jarvis, as well as Baker and Howland, due to the removal of predators from the islands. The Phoenix petrel is known from the Phoenix Islands, but does not currently inhabit Jarvis, though it is thought that they did historically. A recommendation of the Seabird Conservation Plan (2005) is expand efforts to assess habitat suitability and restore populations through translocation to predator-free U.S. islands such as Jarvis. While the physical translocation of species to Jarvis is not being suggested, electronic calling devises are designed, and have been successful, in attracting and establishing nesting seabird colonies to other islands.				

Objective 3c: Develop baseline data and understand sea turtle use of Jarvis.				
Upon CCP approval, monitor hawksbill and green sea turtles to document any nesting sites, all adjacent coral reef and nearshore water foraging sites, and overall population density and distributions.				
Alternatives	Alt A	Alt B	Alt C	Alt D
Objective as written above applies to Alternatives (✓)	✓	✓	✓	✓
Strategies Applied to Achieve Objective	Alt A	Alt B	Alt C	Alt D
Record incidental observations of nearshore turtle use.	✓	✓	✓	✓
Develop and conduct survey of nearshore turtle use.			✓	✓
Develop and conduct survey of other marine areas for turtle use.				✓
Develop partnership with NOAA for study of turtles at Jarvis.		✓	✓	✓

Rationale:
There is currently little information related to use of Jarvis resources by sea turtles, though it is known that they do use refuge habitats. Sea turtles have been photographed in the water during joint Service/NOAA expeditions since 2000. Data collected over the life of this plan would help to establish a baseline understanding of sea turtle populations in the central Pacific.

Objective 3d: Expand baseline information on marine community.				
Upon CCP approval, monitor populations of globally depleted marine species such as giant clams (*Tridacna* sp.), bumphead parrotfish (*Bolbometapon muricatum*), Napoleon wrasses (*Cheilinus undulatus*), large groupers (*Cephalopholis* sp., *Epinephelus* spp., *Variola* spp., etc.), sharks (*Carcharhinus* spp., *Triaenodon* spp., *Negaprion* spp., *Galeocerdo* spp., etc.), and corals (Anthozoa, Hydrozoa) to document their presence/absence and relative abundance on Jarvis.				
Alternatives	Alt A	Alt B	Alt C	Alt D
Objective as written above applies to Alternatives (✓)	✓	✓	✓	✓
Strategies Applied to Achieve Objective	Alt A	Alt B	Alt C	Alt D
Conduct marine surveys such as REA	✓	✓	✓	✓
Solicit partnership for survey of deep slope habitat		✓	✓	✓
Expand marine surveys (REA) efforts to other reef areas surrounding the island				✓
Rationale:				
Many marine species of commercial importance have been globally depleted. Protected areas such as Jarvis still provide sanctuary areas. However, illegal fishing activity has been noted surrounding several Remotes refuges. Jarvis, as well as other remote island refuges provide the opportunity to study and protect the marine ecosystem.				

Objective 3e: Develop baseline scientific information on marine mammal use of Jarvis.				
Within 10 years of CCP approval, increase scientific understanding of marine mammal presence and use of Jarvis marine waters. The desired conditions by which this will be met will be to document all marine mammal use of nearshore waters.				
Alternatives	Alt A	Alt B	Alt C	Alt D
Objective as written above applies to Alternatives (✓)	✓	✓	✓	✓
Strategies Applied to Achieve Objective	Alt A	Alt B	Alt C	Alt D
Incidental observations of marine mammal	✓	✓	✓	✓
Solicit partnership for study of marine mammals at Jarvis		✓	✓	✓
Rationale:				
NOAA, the Service, Oceanic Institute, University of Hawaii, and Bishop Museum marine biologists have collected data on marine species of concern since 2000. Only anecdotal				

information exists on marine mammal use of the waters surrounding Jarvis Island. However, studies elsewhere in the Pacific indicate that waters surrounding small islands may support distinct local populations of marine mammals. It is also important to understand the threats human activity may pose to this important resource (Marine Mammal Commission. pers. comm.).

Goal 4: Protect, maintain, enhance, and preserve the wilderness character of Jarvis's terrestrial and marine communities.

Objective 4a: Protect and maintain wilderness values.				
Upon CCP approval, continue to preserve the wilderness values (e.g. size, naturalness, solitude, supplemental values) of Jarvis. Achievement of this objective will be evaluated by assessing loss or degradation of values that qualified it for potential designation (see Appendix F).				
Alternatives	Alt A	Alt B	Alt C	Alt D
Objective as written above applies to Alternatives (✓)	✓	✓	✓	✓
Strategies Applied to Achieve Objective	Alt A	Alt B	Alt C	Alt D
Use minimum tools necessary to manage refuge resources	✓	✓	✓	✓
Continue to manage Jarvis as wilderness	✓	✓	✓	✓
Monitor values of naturalness and solitude.	✓	✓	✓	✓
Remove debris remaining from military or other past human use, not considered cultural resources.			✓	✓
Rationale:				
Jarvis has been and is currently managed as a wild, natural area due to its remote location, historic lack of human impact, and limited human presence. Areas of Jarvis have been identified as meeting the criteria for a Wilderness Study Area (Appendix F). Completion of the wilderness review process and as appropriate development of a Legislative EIS will be pursued for all Pacific Remote Island Refuges once their CCP's have been completed. Some human generated debris remains from past occupations. Additionally, debris such as discarded fishing nets continuously washes ashore. This debris impinges upon wilderness values. A cultural resource review is required prior to removal of any human debris, identified as a component of Alternatives C and D, which may be considered a cultural resource. In the interim, all areas identified as suitable WSAs would continue to be managed as wilderness. All management activities would be conducted in such a manner as not to detract from the wilderness values identified in the Wilderness Inventory.				

Goal 5: Jarvis's cultural and historic resources are preserved.

Objective 5a: Protect cultural resources.				
Upon CCP approval, continue to protect existing cultural resources. The desired conditions by which this will be met will be to document any change in condition of the Jarvis Light day beacon, or other recognized cultural/historical resource.				
Alternatives	Alt A	Alt B	Alt C	Alt D
Objective as written above applies to Alternatives (✓)	✓	✓	✓	✓
Strategies Applied to Achieve Objective	Alt A	Alt B	Alt C	Alt D
Record incidental observations of condition of cultural resources	✓	✓	✓	✓
Rationale:				
Rationale: Restricting human use of Jarvis would maintain cultural resources by limiting the opportunity for invasive species establishment, and reducing the opportunity for unauthorized collection or disturbance. In order to keep cultural resource sites protected, the locations and descriptions of fragile cultural resources would not be made available to the public.				

Objective 5b: Enhance Knowledge of cultural resources.				
Within 10 years of CCP approval, undertake appropriate surveys to identify important cultural and historical resources.				
Alternatives	Alt A	Alt B	Alt C	Alt D
Objective as written above applies to Alternatives (✓)			✓	✓
Strategies Applied to Achieve Objective	Alt A	Alt B	Alt C	Alt D
Conduct cultural resource survey of island and marine habitat			✓	✓
Conduct basic maintenance of cultural resources (paint, clean surfaces of avian excrement)			✓	✓
Rationale:				
Restricting human use of Jarvis would maintain cultural resources by limiting the opportunity for invasive species establishment, and reducing the opportunity for unauthorized collection or disturbance. In order to keep cultural resource sites protected, the locations and descriptions of fragile cultural resources would not be made available to the public. Any maintenance activity, and establishment of seasonal or annual field camps would require approval from appropriate archeological resource professional (Service's Regional Archeologist).				

Goal 6: An informed, interested, and educated public appreciates remote Pacific Island NWRs wilderness values, cultural and historical resources, and their ecosystems, with special emphasis on seabirds.

Objective 6a: Provide off-site education and interpretation opportunities.				
Within three years of CCP approval, develop an off-site educational opportunity for the public to learn about Pacific Island refuge wilderness values, cultural and historical resources, tropical island ecosystems, seabirds, and coral reefs. The desired conditions by which this will be met will be through publications, educational programs, displays, or other media.				
Alternatives	Alt A	Alt B	Alt C	Alt D
Objective as written above applies to Alternatives (✓)	✓	✓	✓	✓
Strategies Applied to Achieve Objective	Alt A	Alt B	Alt C	Alt D
Develop, with External Affairs office, Honolulu, an interpretative brochure for all remote Pacific Island refuges.		✓	✓	✓
Work with External Affairs office, Honolulu to develop outreach/interpretation strategy.			✓	✓
Rationale:				
While it is important for the public to understand and appreciate the resource values associated with remote island refuges, it is logistically difficult to do this on-site at Jarvis and still protect the island's wildlife, habitats, wilderness values, cultural and historical resources, and visitor's safety. For these reasons, interpretative or educational opportunities for the public to learn and appreciate the values of remote Pacific Island refuges and resources will be provided primarily as off-site programs and interpretative brochures.				

Objective 6b: Increase understanding of impacts of global climate change.				
Within 15 years of CCP approval, increase scientific understanding of the impacts of global climate change on tropical island ecosystems, specifically as these impacts relate to seabird nesting and foraging sites. The desired conditions by which this will be met will be the development of one research project.				
Alternatives	Alt A	Alt B	Alt C	Alt D
Objective as written above applies to Alternatives (✓)			✓	✓
Strategies Applied to Achieve Objective	Alt A	Alt B	Alt C	Alt D
Develop partnership with agency or institution to conduct baseline global climate change investigations			✓	✓
Rationale:				
It is increasingly important to understand the impacts that global climate change might have on central Pacific Ocean islands and the wildlife resources they provide such as				

seabird nesting habitat. In order to determine if management activities are necessary to offset the impacts of global climate change at Jarvis, refuge staff needs a baseline from which to measure future change.

Chapter 3: Affected Environment

3.1 Geographic/Ecosystem Setting

Jarvis Island, located at approximately lat. 0°23' N. and long. 160°01' W is the sixth island and considered to be a western outlier of the 11 Line Islands that stretch from 6°N latitude to 11°S latitude. The Line Islands trend from north to south between longitudes 162° and 150°W. Kingman Reef National Wildlife Refuge anchors the northern end of the archipelago and Flint Island anchors the southern end, about 390 nmi north of Tahiti in French Polynesia. It is included in the Central Pacific subregion of the Polynesian Region of the Pacific Basin. This subregion, the largest of four in the Polynesian Region, is the most remote part of the tropical Pacific and includes only low-lying reef islands, atolls, and submerged reefs. Vegetation patterns are determined by the highly variable but normally low rainfall levels found along the Equator in the central Pacific. In turn, the arid weather and ocean circulation patterns impose limits on floating seed plant dispersal strategies. Jarvis falls in the central Pacific dry zone with rainfall less than 40 inches per year, and thus "cannot support any forest or closed woody vegetation" (Mueller-Dombois and Fosberg 1998). The nearest landmass is Kiritimati (Christmas) Island, 184 nmi to the north. Three of the Line Islands are possessions of the United States (U.S.), all being administered as units of the NWRS. Jarvis, and Kingman Reef are both unincorporated U.S. territories, while Palmyra Atoll is the only U.S. possession considered an incorporated U.S. Territory, meaning that it enjoys all the legal privileges provided by the U.S. Constitution. The remaining eight Line Islands are under the jurisdiction of the Republic of Kiribati; their capital is Tarawa, located in the Gilbert Islands 1,621 nmi to the West.

3.2 Climate

General climate and related oceanographic conditions in the central Equatorial Pacific
The climate associated with Jarvis Island can be generalized as being arid, warm, and tropical with moderate breezes and light to moderate rainfall. Although differences in climate exist among the islands, climate-monitoring stations are not readily available in the equatorial Pacific. Consequently, current site-specific data is lacking for most central Pacific locations, or has only been collected for a short period of time. Vitousek, et al. (1980), recorded meteorological observations at Jarvis Island from 1974 to 1980 and these data will serve as the basis for this summary.

There are several climatic factors that influence weather on Jarvis: trade winds, rainfall, and oceanic currents. Trade winds are surface winds that typically dominate airflow in tropical regions and predominate from the East at Jarvis between 13 to16 miles per hour. Atmospheric pressure gradients range from high pressure areas located near lat. 30° N. and lat. 30° S., to the low pressure band located near lat. 5° N., driving both the northeast and southeast trade winds. This area of low pressure located just north of the Equator is referred to as the 'doldrums' or the Intertropical Convergence Zone (ITCZ) and lacks these prevailing trade winds because they converge and rise upward.

Solar heating also allows the moist air mass of the ITCZ to rise, thus cooling the air mass and producing a band of heavy precipitation several degrees to either side of the ITCZ (Wallace and Hobbs 1977). Jarvis's position near the Equator places it outside this band of heavy precipitation. Changes in these typical patterns occur seasonally and during periodic events known as the El Niño Southern Oscillation (ENSO). During an ENSO event, the ITCZ shifts south and east toward unusually warmer waters. At other equatorial islands, this shift typically leads to lighter wind speeds and more rainfall (USFWS 2001, USFWS 1998a) but Jarvis did not have an increase the in rainfall during the ENSO events of 1974 to 1976 that Kiritimati and Tabuaeran (Fanning) Islands experienced (Vitousek et al. 1980).

Prevailing ocean currents surrounding Jarvis Island also influence weather patterns on the island by moderating the surrounding surface air temperatures. These currents, except the Equatorial Undercurrent (EUC), and North Equatorial Countercurrent (NECC), also roughly mimic the direction of the trade winds. The eastward-flowing NECC is a relatively narrow surface current that seasonally meanders between 5° and 10° North latitude, flows counter to the major westward-flowing currents of the northern and southern hemispheres, and is situated just below the ITCZ (USFWS 2001). In a sense, the NECC is a return flow of surface seawater running down-slope back towards the eastern Pacific because of the lack of trade winds that would otherwise drag surface waters in the opposite direction. Jarvis lays 400 nm south of the most southerly approach of the NECC and is rarely directly influenced by the current.

The westward-flowing current lying north of the NECC is known as the North Equatorial Current (NEC) and is not known to influence current and weather patterns near Jarvis. Just south of the NECC is the westward-flowing South Equatorial Current (SEC). Jarvis is most always within the flow regime of the SEC.

Jarvis Island also lies in the path of the subsurface easterly flowing Equatorial Undercurrent (EUC) also referred to as the Cromwell Current. As the EUC strikes the submerged western slopes of Jarvis Island, nutrient rich waters are deflected upward, enriching the primary productivity of the surface waters surrounding Jarvis. These upwelling waters from the EUC are slightly cooler than adjacent sea surface waters and may moderate the effects of localized and periodic sea surface warming events. Variations in the upwelling that cause it to be strongest during boreal spring are caused by variations in wind levels over various time scales (Gove et al., 2006).

Jarvis Island climate data

The nearest currently operating weather station to Jarvis is the Kiritimati weather station, located at lat. 1° 52' N., long. 157°20' W., or roughly 184 nmi north of Jarvis (USFWS 1998a). This station reports average total monthly rainfall of approximately 3 inches ranging from 0 to 20 inches per month with precipitation consistent throughout the year (NOAA 1991) except for increases during ENSO events.

3.3 *Global Climate Change*

Background

Recent decades have brought increased awareness of the changing global environment and the implications this may have on ecological processes. Global warming, sea level rise, and change in chemical concentrations in the world's oceans reflect this change. These changes are being brought about by three factors: increasing concentrations of carbon dioxide and other gasses in the atmosphere commonly referred to as the greenhouse effect; alterations in the biogeochemistry of the global nitrogen cycle; and ongoing land use and land cover change with change in land use being considered the single most important component of global change affecting ecological systems (Vitousek, 1994). While there is considerable debate regarding the cause and the ultimate impact these changes will have on earth's environment, there are several areas of impact that have been well documented. The three areas of impact linked to global climate change, which may have the greatest potential effect on Jarvis, and other central Pacific islands are coral bleaching, sea level rise and oceanic chemical composition change.

Vitousek (1994) reported, "Changes in both climate and biological diversity are known with less certainty than are changes in CO_2 concentrations, global biogeochemistry or land use". Because temperature is more variable both spatially and temporally than CO_2 concentration, it is difficult to separate human-caused vs. natural background variation. However, it is certain that increasing concentrations of CO_2 and other greenhouse gasses will cause increasing climate change (Vitousek, 1994).

The equatorial locale for Jarvis places it near the path of anomalous water current and surface wind conditions during ENSO events, but the paucity of weather and oceanographic data at Jarvis renders it difficult to assess the impacts and trends of global climate change at the island. The upward deflection of cool subsurface waters into shallow water by the upwelling effects of the EUC further complicates an assessment of climate change effects, because this phenomenon has been rarely reported outside of the three equatorial refuges (Howland, Baker, Jarvis).

Coral Bleaching

Above normal mean sea surface temperatures have been shown to cause bleaching and mortality in corals both in nature and in the laboratory with bleaching generally occurring in shallower waters (Floros et al. 2004). Other variables have also been implicated in bleaching and mortality events, including, extended periods of high temperatures, low wind velocity, clear skies, calm seas, low rainfall, high rainfall, salinity changes, high turbidity or acute pollution. Smith and Buddemeier (1992) state: "Reef damage from anthropogenic environmental degradation (nutrient runoff, siltation, overexploitation) is widespread, represents a much greater threat than climate change in the near future, and can reinforce the negative effects of climate change". Floros et al. (2004) goes on to note that, "The causes of coral bleaching are debatable, but widely thought to be the result of a variety of stresses, both natural and human-induced, that cause the degeneration and the loss of the colored zooxanthellae from the coral tissues."

Field observation of corals at Jarvis during five separate expeditions from 2000-2006 indicate that corals appear to be recovering from a bleaching event that took place during the previous few years (1997-1998). Corals continued to recover based upon observations during all subsequent (post 2000) visits. Although coral bleaching was predicted to occur at Jarvis in 2003 based upon NOAA satellite based temperature and wind data, no evidence of bleaching was reported there during the early 2004 and 2006 visits (Maragos 2000-2006, unpublished data). One possible explanation is that the cool upwelling waters of the EUC are buffering the effects of the otherwise warmer seawater temperatures at the island.

Tudhope (2000) sampled 6 cores obtained from 2 large,3-4 meter *Porites* coral heads at Jarvis in 1999 to track sea surface temperature and coral growth rates over several or more decades using stable oxygen isotope as a measure of Sea Surface Temperature. He found a good correlation between this measure and the NINO3.4 Index, which is one of the most widely used and reliable indicators of the status of ENSO. The results of their work at Jarvis and at four other tropical sites in the Line and Cook Islands contributed to demonstrating linkages between the tropics and the North Pacific over hundreds of years (D'arrigo et al 2005). Hawaii Undersea Research Laboratory (HURL) submersible dives at Jarvis in July 2005 revealed many deep-water corals, and samples of some were taken for climate change and paleo-climate analyses (Rob Dunbar et al. 2005). The results of these analyses are not yet available.

Sea Level Rise
While global temperature is projected to rise by 3.6 to 9°F and sea level to rise by more than 31.5 inches during the next two centuries, sea levels have fluctuated by an order of 328 feet over the past 18,000 years as natural background variation and thawing out from the last ice age (Michener et al. 1997). Contributions to sea level rise by climate change are ice-sheet melting, alpine glacier melting and thermal expansion of the sea. Sea levels have risen by 4-8 inches during the past century (Michener et al. 1997). The Intergovernmental Panel on Climate Change (IPCC 2001) predicted a sea level rise of 3.5 inches to 34.6 inches by the year 2100 unless greenhouse gas emissions were reduced substantially. They also suggested that continuing greenhouse gas emissions could trigger polar ice-cap melting after 2100 accompanied by sea level rise greater than 16 feet. More recent modeling indicates that melting could occur faster than the IPCC predicted (Overpeck, et al. 2006).

Evidence also suggests that the world's oceans are regionally divisible with regard to historic fluctuations in sea level. Localized variations in subsidence and emergence of the sea floor and plate-tectonics activity prevent extrapolations in sea level fluctuations and trends between different regions. Thus, it may not be possible to discuss uniform changes in sea level on a global scale, or the magnitude of greenhouse gas-forced changes as these changes may vary regionally (Michener et al. 1997). As an example, tide gauge records on the Atlantic coast indicate a sea level rise of .06 to .16 in/year over the past century, whereas, they have indicated a .35 to .39 in/year increase along the Gulf coast of the United States (Michener et al. 1997).

Increases in sea level may also affect low-lying equatorial islands and atolls. Shoreline erosion and salt water intrusion into subsurface freshwater aquifers have been noted throughout the Pacific (Shea et al. 2001). Due to the deep marine slopes directly adjacent to Jarvis Island, increases in sea level could significantly erode shorelines and overall island surface area since opportunities for accretion of lands do not exist. Data related to sea level near Jarvis Island was not found in the literature reviewed for this plan.

Oceanic Chemical Concentration Change

Glacial and interglacial periods during Earth's history, cycle repeatedly with low and high concentrations of carbon dioxide (as measured from deep Antarctic ice cores). However, recent increases fall outside the range of peak prehistoric carbon dioxide levels. The rate of increase is also 5 to 10 times more rapid than any of the sustained changes in the ice-core record (Vitousek, 1994). Carbon dioxide levels have increased from 280 to 355 μL/L since 1800, a level of increase otherwise never reported during the past 160,000 years. Data suggest this increase is linked to fossil fuel combustion and not deforestation (Vitousek, 1994).

Change in carbon dioxide levels will increase the partial pressure of carbon dioxide in seawater, thus reducing the over saturation of aragonite, a form of calcium carbonate that is the major building block for coral reefs (Vitousek, 1994). The result of this is uncertain but is thought to reduce the rate at which corals can deposit calcium carbonate, thus reducing the rate at which coral reefs will be able to keep up with any increases in sea level.

It should also be noted that chemical composition changes in the atmosphere may also affect terrestrial ecosystems. For instance, the quantity of nitrogen available to organisms affects species composition and productivity. Increase in nitrogen can alter species composition by favoring those plant species that respond to nitrogen increases (Vitousek, 1994). Increased carbon dioxide can also impact photosynthetic rates in plants, change plant species composition, lower nutrient levels, and lower weight gain by herbivores.

Summary

Coral bleaching has not been documented at Jarvis but likely occurred in the late 1990s. The buffering effects of the EUC may contribute to corals being less susceptible to bleaching events. Sea level rise is well documented throughout the world's oceans, but local data are lacking. Thus, the magnitude of changes in sea level and the impact this may have on Jarvis Island ecosystems is currently speculative. The localized impact of changes in atmospheric and oceanic chemical concentrations is also unknown. While many of the impacts of global climate change currently cannot be documented at Jarvis Island, the opportunity exists for Jarvis, and other equatorial Pacific island refuges to contribute information to improve global predictions and provide a central Pacific baseline to document changes primarily not affected by human impacts such as land use and pollution.

3.4 Geology and Soils

Jarvis Island is a low-lying, nearly level island with a slightly depressed central area surrounded by a narrow shallow fringing reef. The submarine slopes descend steeply to great depths beyond the fringing reefs. Surface deposits on the island consist of calcareous sands and coral rock. The central depression is probably the remnants of an ancient lagoon and the result of the combined effects of guano mining more than a century ago and wave action depositing sand rocks and boulders around the island's fringe to an elevation of 10-23 feet above sea level (Keating, 1992). The island was likely formed as a result of submarine volcanic activity and changes in the earth's crust caused by continental tectonic plate movement, including emergence of a high volcanic island, its later subsidence, reef accretion, and its gradual northwesterly drift away from the East

Pacific Rise over the past 50-80 million years. Although scientists since Darwin (1842) have been pondering seamount, island, and atoll formation in the Pacific since the mid-1800s, the specifics of how Jarvis Island was formed have not been specifically investigated, although they would likely follow the general sequence first postulated by Darwin.

The dominant theory of atoll formation states that islands form in deep tropical oceans as a result of underwater volcanoes that grow to the surface to form high volcanic islands, giving coral polyps a foundation to grow upon and form reefs fringing the island. In time, the volcano becomes dormant, and its mass pushes down on the earth's crust causing it and its island to subside and shrink in size, while its fringing reefs continue to grow upward and maintain proximity to the sea surface. Coral reefs, originally fringing the edges of a large island, become a barrier reef around larger islands outlining the contour of the original coastline, with a lagoon occupying the space vacated by the shrinking island. Eventually, further subsidence causes the island to disappear completely from the lagoon leaving behind an atoll. However, for small islands such as Jarvis, lagoons may not have formed at latter stages, and continued subsidence has left only a small low reef island in its wake. Based upon deep drilling through the atolls in the Marshall Islands in the 1940s and 1950s, it is believed that these processes occurred well before the beginning of the last ice age (approximately 115,000 years ago) and encompassed more than 50- 60 million years and up to several thousand feet of reef growth equal to the degree of subsidence over that time span. In addition, it is hypothesized that changes in sea level associated with the end of the last ice age and the deposition of highly permeable coralline limestone (calcium carbonate) derived from the remains of marine organisms likely contributed to the carbonate platform that characterizes the contemporary geologic structure of Jarvis Island.

The entire western or leeward beach of the island is sandy and low, while the eastern side, constantly pounded by waves generated by the trade winds, is higher, more abrupt, and covered with coral rubble and sandstone slabs. There is no pronounced beach crest or central basin (dried up lagoon) typically found on some larger low-lying reef islands. Soils of low-lying atolls in the Pacific frequently consist of accumulated organic matter, guano, pumice or other transported material on top of a calcareous sand or limestone substratum (Morrison 1990). The soil of Jarvis Island is composed of coral fragments and light brown coral sand with a low percentage of organic matter.

Hutchinson (1950) concluded that phosphates accumulate preferentially on islands, such as Howland, Baker and Jarvis Islands, that are situated in climatic dry belts used by large populations of seabirds. Deposits of phosphate-rich soils have formed over time from guano deposited on the island by fish-eating seabirds. Mild acids formed from the decomposition of organic matter carry the guano downward in the soil to limestone soil layers were acids are neutralized and calcium phosphate accumulated from the chemical changes. In addition, when guano-beds are exposed to rain their soluble constituents are removed and the insoluble matter is left behind. The soluble phosphates washed out of the guano may also become fixed to the coral sand and limestone by the process described above. The calcium phosphate rocks and soil occur among the sedimentary strata and were the principal sources of phosphate targeted for commercial fertilizer and military use during the guano mining period between 1861 and 1891(see Chapter 3.15). Even after the guano mining era, the soil profile still contained heavy guano deposits (Christophersen 1927).

3.5 Hydrology

No information is available on the subsurface hydrology of Jarvis Island. However, its small size and prevailing arid rainfall conditions would not likely result in the formation of a drinkable groundwater lens. During staff visits to Jarvis, potable water is carried in containers to the island for short visits, and could be produced on-site via reverse osmosis technology for prolonged visits, just as it is now produced for permanent field stations at other remote Pacific Island NWRs.

3.6 Air and Water Quality

Due to the lack of human presence, oceanic and air quality are expected to be good and lacking in pollutants. The acoustic environment at Jarvis is completely natural without any anthropogenic noise except during periodic visits. On the island, dominant natural sounds include the wind, calls of seabird and shorebirds, and seawater lapping on the shoreline with wave action crashing further offshore on the outer reef margin. Underwater the dominant sounds are wave action and surge striking the reef slopes and the sounds of thousands of feeding and moving invertebrates and fish.

3.7 Environmental Contaminants

The most recent human activity at Jarvis Island that resulted in possible environmental contamination occurred between 1974 and 1980. The NORPAX Line Islands Monitoring Experiment included an automated weather station at Jarvis that consisted of a various meteorological and oceanographic sensors, a small hut housing the electronics box, a 100 watt FSK radio transmitter, radio and sensor towers, wind generators, solar panels, primary and secondary batteries, and power control circuits. Power for the station was stored in 18-volt lead-acid batteries and radio transmission powered by 12 volt batteries (Vitousek et al., 1980). At least some of these batteries and some of the other metallic objects were left behind on Jarvis at the end of this research.

Other periods of human occupation at Jarvis include an 18 month occupation of Jarvis from 1 July 1957 to 31 Dec 1958 by a party of oceanographers from Scripps Institution of Oceanography during the International Geophysical Year. They left a house in 1958, which is no longer standing. Panala'au colonists occupied the island from 1935 to 1942 and as many as 80 guano miners at any given time worked there from 1858 to 1879. The guano mining process itself does not result in harmful tailings so only substances that may have been left by the miners or subsequently by the colonists might qualify as environmental contamination on the refuge. The east end of Jarvis was shelled by a Japanese submarine in 1942. A large storm from the north in 1958 washed away practically all evidence of the guano miners and the Panala'au colonists from the Millersville landing area.

3.8 Terrestrial Vegetation and Habitats

Jarvis Island is vegetated with grasses, herbaceous plants, and shrubs. Only strand species able to survive long periods of drought and irregular opportunities to reproduce during the infrequent wet years of the ENSO persist here. By 1924 when Christophersen (1927) did the first thorough survey of Jarvis Island's vegetation, there had already been approximately a century of visits by Europeans and guano miners. Despite this traffic and the potential for introductions, Christophersen found a very depauperate flora consisting of 6 native species (*Lepturus repens, Eragrostis whitneyi, Sesuvium portulacastrum, Boerhavia tetrandra., Portulaca lutea, Tribulus cistoides, Other plants currently surviving such as *Abutifolium indicum,* and *Sida fallax* were most likely accidentally introduced by the guano miners. Still other plants were purposefully introduced through the years, perhaps even repeatedly, but do not persist. (see Appendix B). On a short visit in 2004, only 7 species of plants were located (Rauzon and Wegmann 2004). It is likely that seeds of additional species are regularly washing up on the beach and then dying back as conditions become too dry or high surf washes the plant away. Table B-3, Appendix B, lists all the plant species of Jarvis Island, and the most recent information about current presence or absence.

The structure of the plant community is grassland and low herbaceous cover. The *Sida* and *Abutilon* in the interior serve as important nesting and roosting habitat for the red-footed booby and cover for wintering bristle-thighed curlews. Great frigatebirds and white terns also prefer to nest above the ground on the few shrubs available, but all the other species nest directly on the ground. Shrubs and rock piles also provide shade and daytime cover for the numerous land hermit crabs, *Coenobita perlatus* that inhabit Jarvis Island.

3.9 Terrestrial Wildlife

Seabirds, shorebirds, lizards, vegetation, insects, crabs, and invasive rats and feral cats were observed and studied at Jarvis Island during the current century. The Service subsequently eradicated cats from the island that enabled several nesting seabird species to re-colonize the island.

3.9.1 Seabirds and Land Mammals

There are no native land mammals at Jarvis Island. Numerically dominant vertebrates are seabirds and migratory shorebirds. Earliest ornithological surveys at Jarvis Island took place long after the introduction of the Polynesian rat, *Rattus exulans,* so the composition of the avian community prior to human contact can only be surmised by looking at other islands in the Phoenix and Line Archipelago that did not suffer the invasion of rats. The findings of the ornithologist on the Whippoorwill Expedition of 1924 have never been published. The only ornithological records prior to 1963, when scientists from the Smithsonian Institution visited eight times between 1963 and 1965, are those of Harold Kirby (1925) who visited in 1924 and mentions only 6 species of the large Pelecaniforms breeding. Table B-4 in Appendix B lists species and estimates of numbers for seabird species on all visits since 1973. Jarvis Island falls into Bird Conservation Region (BCR) 68 along with all the other island territories of the U.S.

Cats were introduced to Jarvis sometime during period between 1935 – 1942. The scientists of the POBSP found nine species of seabirds breeding at Jarvis in 1963 (Clapp, R.B, 1967). Cats were finally removed in 1990 (Rauzon, M. J., 1990) and since then there has been a remarkable recovery of almost the entire seabird community. Most spectacular has been the rapid resurgence of blue noddies. There were none found breeding untill 1982 when one nest was located. By 2004 Rauzon and Wegmann (2004) observed 650 birds making Jarvis now one of the largest blue noddy colonies in the world. The recovery of this species as well as the re-colonization of 3 shearwater species at Jarvis coincides with the continuing destruction of the formerly enormous seabird colony at Kiritimati as more and more citizens of Kiribati are settled there. Jarvis has consequently become the largest seabird colony in the Central Pacific. The three most numerous breeding species at Jarvis are the sooty tern (*Onychoprion fuscatus*), brown noddy (*Anous stolidus*), and masked booby, (*Sula dactylatra*).

Several species of concern exist or have the potential to exist on Jarvis. The Phoenix petrel (*Pterodroma alba*) is considered a bird of National Conservation Concern by the Service and is listed by the IUCN as Vulnerable. The Polynesian storm-petrel (*Nesofregetta fuliginosa*) and blue noddy (*Procelsterna cerulean*) are Birds of Conservation Concern at the regional level (USFWS 2005). Both the Phoenix petrel and the Polynesian storm-petrel probably occurred at Jarvis Island prior to the introduction of rats.

3.9.2 Shorebirds

Species occurrence and counts of the four migratory shorebird species recorded from Jarvis Island are displayed in Table B-4, Appendix B. The most common migrants wintering at Jarvis are the Pacific golden plover (*Pluvialis fulva*) and bristle-thighed curlew (*Numenius tahitiensis*). All four shorebird species are considered species of High Concern in the national conservation priority scheme for shorebirds (Engilis and Naughton 2004). All of the species are also labeled as high concern in the Birds of Conservation Concern in BCR 68 (U.S. Fish and Wildlife Service. 2002). These islands provide crucial wintering habitat and may serve as rest-stops for arctic-breeding shorebirds wintering farther south in the Pacific Islands.

3.9.3 Reptiles

Only one species of terrestrial reptile has been reported from Jarvis Island, a gecko, most likely the mourning gecko (*Lepidodactylus lugubris*). This species was documented in the stomach of a cat at Jarvis (Kirkpatrick and Rauzon, 1986) and may have served as alternate prey for cats when they were present on Jarvis Island.

3.9.4 Invertebrates (crabs and insects)

Jarvis Island is home to a large number of the land crab, *Coenobita perlatus*. Their large biomass plays a dominant role in terrestrial food webs on the island where they consume a wide variety of organic matter of all types. Other terrestrial arthropods and mollusks are very poorly known. Recent observations, but not collections, during visits by Service biologists include house flies, small ants, moths and millers, butterflies, and spiders. Kirkpatrick and Rauzon

(1986) compared food habits of feral cats at Howland and Jarvis Islands and while there were crickets, cockroaches and Tenebrionid beetles in the stomach of Jarvis cats (n=73), no insect remains were found in a smaller sample (n=5) of Howland Island cats.

3.10 Marine Habitats, Fish, and Wildlife

3.10.1 Previous surveys

Before regular marine assessment and monitoring efforts began in 2000, marine scientists visited Jarvis to collect fish, corals, and perhaps other reef life, but there were no systematic surveys of the reefs accomplished or reported in the literature. Five sets of recent surveys through early 2006 have been accomplished in cooperation with the NOAA Pacific Islands Fisheries Science Center (PIFSC) and their research vessels (*Townsend Cromwell, Oscar Elton Sette,* and *Hi'ialakai*), primarily through the sponsorship of the Center's Coral Reef Ecosystem Division (CRED)(R. Brainard, per. comm.). The surveys since 2000 are of several types including: oceanographic data collection, towed diver surveys, rapid ecological assessments (REA) at stationary sites, and collections of marine animals and plants for identification and description in the lab. The Service with assistance from CRED established three permanently-marked transects to document trends in corals and some macro-invertebrates over time since 2000-2002. In addition, The University of Hawaii/NOAA sponsored HURL program accomplished several deep submersible dives at Jarvis in July 2005 to depths of 3,000 feet, and reported large populations of fish and deep corals off the west side of the island where the EUC impinges on the submarine slopes of the island

Despite these intense efforts, several important habitats at Jarvis have not been adequately surveyed. Windward (north and east facing) reefs were inaccessible during most visits because of tradewind generated waves close to the reef and onshore winds that would push the dive skiffs too close to the reefs. Moreover, due to safety concerns, dives have generally been limited to depths of 60 feet and one hour duration. Because of these limitations, some important habitats are still poorly sampled and deep slope habitats (164 to 3,000 feet) within the refuge remain mostly unexplored, except for the 2005 HURL dives and 2006 acquisition of high resolution bathymetry of Jarvis Island NWR from Multi-Beam™ surveys (S. Ferguson, per. comm.) and substantial oceanographic data (R. Brainard, per. comm.).

3.10.2 Submergent Habitats

Jarvis Island's shallow marine benthic habitats consist of fringing reef crests, shallow back reefs, steep fore reefs, spurs-and-grooves, and small reef terraces, the last two habitats are restricted to the windward (east side) of the island. In addition, shallow short channels may have been blasted through the narrow fringing reef during the pre-World War II era to facilitate small boat access between the shoreline and ocean off the south and west sides of the island. The deep slope habitats below depths of 60 feet have not been surveyed by divers, although remotely operated vehicles (ROVs) have been launched to collect video and camera based data. Pelagic habitats occur further offshore beyond the influence of upwelling and nearshore oceanographic processes. Nearshore habitats include distinct upwelling zones off the west side of the island and oligotrophic waters off the windward reefs. The PIFSC has conducted oceanographic research off the island to contrast the difference between nutrient rich upwelling zones and the ambient nutrient poor ocean conditions outside areas of upwelling currents.

3.10.3 Reef Life

The dominant reef life that has been studied during post 1997 expeditions include, benthic algae (Peter Vroom, Kim Paige, per. comm.) corals and anemones (John Schmerfeld, Jim Maragos, Bernardo Vargas, and Jean Kenyon, per. comm.), other reef invertebrates (Scott Godwin, Dwayne Minton, and Robin Newbold, per. comm.), and reef fishes (Mundy et al 2002., Ed DeMartini, Bruce Mundy, Brian Zgliczynski, Brian Green, Richard Wass, Alan Friedlander, Stephanie Holzwarth, and others, per. comm.). At the time of this CCP, only data from coral, algae, and pre-2003 fish surveys were available for review and compilation, and the algae and non-coral invertebrate analyses are not complete enough to provide compilations.

The giant clam (*Tridacna maxima*) is abundant Jarvis Island and is listed under the Convention on International Trade in Endangered Species of Wild Fauna and Flora (CITES). Also found on Jarvis, the humphead wrasse (*Cheilinus undulates*) is also listed under CITES and designated as Endangered by the International Union for the Conservation of Nature (IUCN).

3.10.4 Corals

Coral diversity at Jarvis Island
Five coral surveys completed at Jarvis from 2000-2006 have documented 50 species and 20 genera of coral, all but 2 of which are stony coral species (see Appendix B, Table B-1). Calm sea conditions allowed the March 2006 REA team to survey several sites off the north and east sides, providing more complete coverage than has been accomplished during any prior visit to Jarvis. Nine 2006 transect surveys accounted for 14 of the 22 genera reported from Jarvis, although 5 genera (*Montipora, Pocillopora, Pavona, Distichopora,* and *Millepora*) accounted for more than 95% of the corals (Figure 3.1). No new genera and species of corals were reported during the 2006 visit. The normally dominant coral genera of *Acropora* and *Porites* were low in numbers although many of the *Porites* colonies were large. The coral fauna at Jarvis is unusual in being low in diversity compared to that of the neighboring Line Islands surveyed during the past several decades. Jarvis's geographic isolation, lack of protected lagoon habitats and small size compared to the other islands may be responsible for this anomaly. Mean generic richness was low at all REA sites ranging from 5 to 9 genera per 50m2 transect area. The eastern and northern (windward) reef sites showed slightly higher generic richness but lower overall abundance.

Figure 3.1 Percent of Coral Genus Reported During March 2006 Surveys, Jarvis Island NWR. (after Maragos 2006).

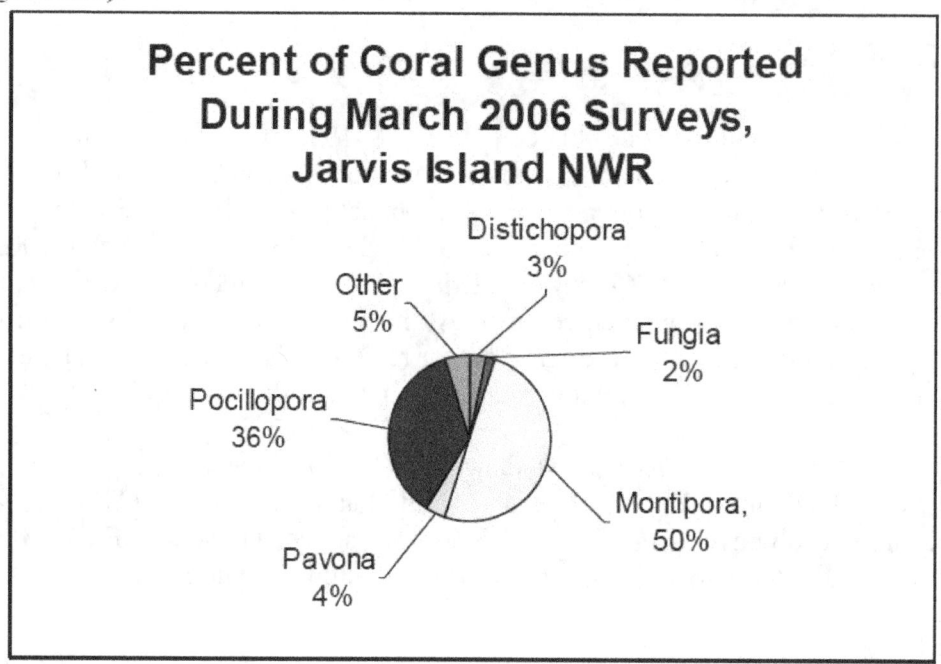

Coral populations

Figures 3.2 and 3.3 summarize the characteristics of the coral populations at the nine 2006 Jarvis sites. A total of 3,237 corals were counted on the transect sites, but there were differences among the sites. The frequency of corals (mean number per m2) was lowest at windward sites varying from 2 to 4 corals per m2. Coral frequency values were highest on the south and west sides of the island with frequencies there ranging from 8 to 13 corals per m2. These sites along with a northwest corner site also supported the largest coral colonies and the same sites and showed higher mean diameter levels for corals. Jarvis is exposed to large northwest swells due to its more westerly position relative to its northern Line Island neighbors, which may impede coral development. The REA sites protected from both these swells and the southeasterly trade winds appear to support larger and more numerous corals, although windward coral communities appear to be more diverse.

Changes in coral populations over time

Data from the 2004 REA surveys were available for 3 sites to offer comparisons to 2006 surveys at the same sites. In all cases coral populations were more abundant and diverse in 2006 compared to 2004. Many more corals and higher frequencies were reported at all sites in 2006. For example, 2004 frequency values ranged from 1 to 2.5 corals per m2, but ranged from 2 to 7 corals per m2 in 2006. Many smaller size classes were more numerous in 2006, although one larger size class (41 to 80 cm in diameter) was more abundant at the sites in 2004. Generic diversity increased from 3 to 4 genera in 2004 to 5 to 8 genera in 2006. Preliminary results from the analysis of permanent quadrat data at site JAR-4P off the south side of Jarvis reveal dramatic increases in corals from 2000 to 2006. Overall, corals appear healthy and growing at Jarvis sites based upon diversity and population parameters. The corals of Jarvis may be rebounding from a global warming and bleaching event of the late 1990s.

Figure 3.2 Size class distributions of corals at 9 REA sites, Jarvis Island NWR 2006.

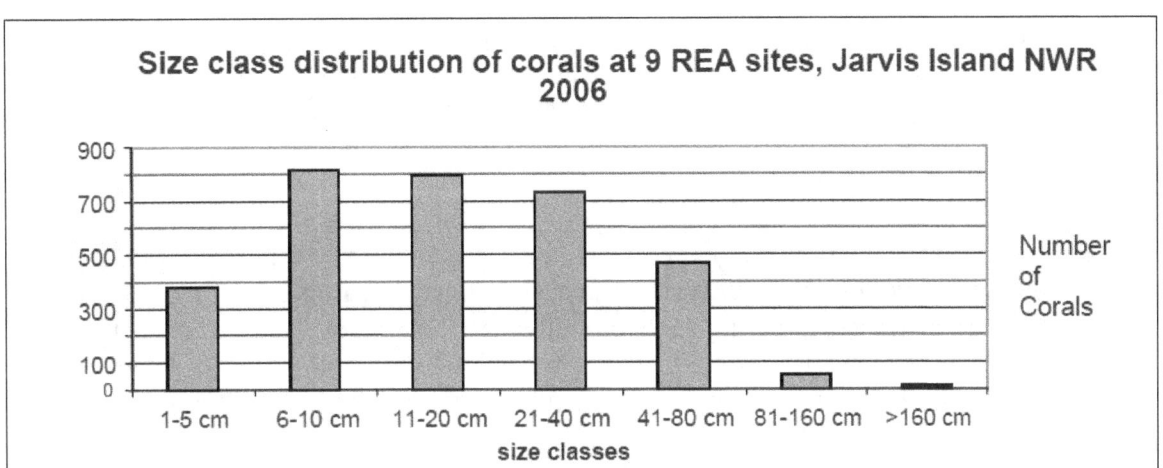

Figure 3.3 Changes in the number of corals per age class between 2000 & 2006 at site 4P, Jarvis Island NWR.

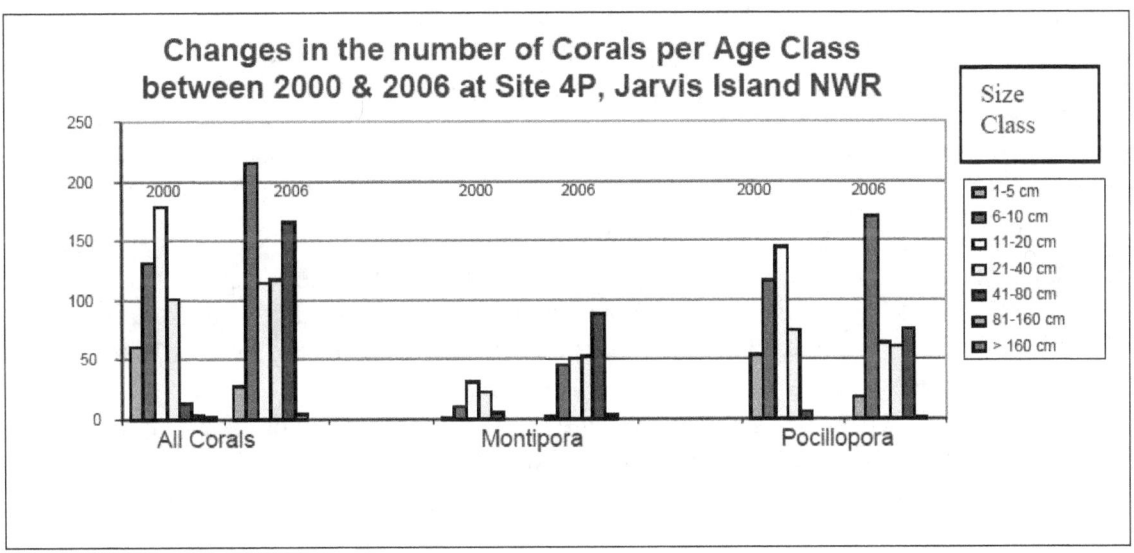

3.10.5 Nearshore Fish

There are approximately 277 species of reef fish known from Jarvis Island reefs (Mundy et al 2002; Table B-2). This compares with 247 species from Baker Island and 342 species from Howland Island by the same investigators. There were disparities among the fish faunas of each of the islands, with some fish families and genera common at one island and other fish families and genera at the two other islands. Possible explanations for these differences may be that sampling and survey intensities may be insufficient and different between the three islands, or that geographic isolation may result in differential recruitment rates between the three islands. Fish well represented at Jarvis included sharks, groupers, damselfish, wrasses, blennies, and surgeon fishes. Also common were rays, eels, soldierfish, scorpionfish, cardinalfish, snappers, goatfish, butterflyfish, angelfish, hawkfish, parrotfish, and triggerfish were common.

Reef fish populations at Jarvis appeared very abundant, healthy, and diverse with little indication of unauthorized harvest (Maragos, per. comm.). The upwelling phenomenon off the west side of Jarvis seemed especially strong during the six visits there since 2000 and fish populations may be benefiting from nutrient-subsidized productivity from the upwelling currents, resulting in large diverse populations of many families of fish.

The fact that the disparities for the coral genera did not track in the same direction as for the fish families (fewer coral genera vs. more fish abundance and variety at Jarvis), reinforces the hypothesis that geographic isolation may lead to biodiversity heterogeneity based on chance and differential recruitment success. Geographic isolation would require both corals and reef fish to rely more on local recruitment vis-à-vis external recruitment. The latter would likely play a much larger role where reefs and islands are larger and closer together and result in similar biodiversity characteristics.

3.10.6 Marine Mammals

Very little information is available on marine mammal populations in the vicinity of Jarvis. However, on most visits to Jarvis Island, a group of approximately 40 bottle-nosed dolphins (*Tursiops truncatus*) appears as the ship approaches the island. Formal quantitative surveys of marine mammal distribution and abundance have not been undertaken at Jarvis.

3.10.7 Pelagic Wildlife

The estimated millions of seabirds breeding at Jarvis are primarily pelagic feeders that obtain the fish and squid they consume by associating with schools of large predatory fish such as tuna and billfish (Fefer et al. 1984). While both predatory fish and seabirds are capable of foraging throughout their pelagic ranges (which encompass the entire tropical ocean), seabirds are most successful at feeding their young when they can find schools of predatory fish within easy commuting range of the breeding colonies. Recently fledged birds, inexperienced in this complex and demanding style of foraging, rely on abundant and local food resources to survive while they learn to locate and capture prey.

Ashmole and Ashmole (1967) and Boehlert (1993) suggest that the circulation cells and wake eddies found downstream of oceanic islands may concentrate plankton and therefore enhance productivity near islands. Higher productivity in turn results in greater abundance of baitfish, thus allowing locally higher tuna populations. Johannes (1981) describes the daily migrations of skipjack tuna and yellowfin tuna to and from the waters near islands and banks. Protection of these tunas near seabird colonies enhances the ability of birds to provide adequate food for their offspring. Wake eddies also concentrate the larvae of many reef fishes and other reef organisms and serve to keep them close to reefs, enhancing survivorship of larvae and recruitment of juveniles and adults back to the reefs. For at least 3 seabird species breeding at Jarvis (brown noddies, white terns, and brown boobies), high proportions (33–56 percent) of their diet originates from the surrounding coral reef ecosystem when compared to other areas where their diet has been studied. (Ashmole and Ashmole 1967; Harrison et al. 1983; King 1970; Diamond 1978). Large numbers of blue noddies may also be taking advantage of cold productive upwelling currents near Jarvis to forage close to the nesting colony (Rauzon and Wegmann, 2004).

3.11 Threatened and Endangered Species

Species listed under the Endangered Species Act documented to use Jarvis include the threatened green sea turtle (*Chelonia mydas*) and endangered hawksbill turtle (*Eretmochelys imbricata*). Very little information is available on sea turtle populations at Jarvis. However, both species have been observed and photographed foraging in the shallow water near the island.

3.12 Invasive Species

Human activities at Jarvis Island have resulted in various non-native species being introduced including the house cat (*Felis catus*), the Polynesian rat (*Rattus exulans*), the House mouse (*Mus musculus),* various ant and cockroach species, and plants such as pandanus (*Pandanus* sp), coconut (*Cocos nucifera*), ilima (*Sida fallax*), and Indian mallow (*Abutilon indicum*). Cats introduced in 1937 were eliminated in 1990. The rats were documented as early as 1854 and in many accounts were described as extremely abundant. Sometime after 1938, they disappeared and have not been recorded since. House mice are abundant during wetter years. Of the plants introduced by humans, only Ilima and Indian mallow have persisted.

3.13 Wilderness Resources

Jarvis remains in a wilderness state in terms of its biota, seascape, and landscape except the Jarvis Light day beacon aid to navigation, some discarded batteries from the International Geophysical Year camp, excavations and pits left behind from the guano mining era, and a small section of the reef blasted for a boat passage during the guano mining era. Abandoned anchors and chain may occur near the western boat passage. However, the collective contribution of these detractions is minor compared to the otherwise overwhelming wilderness character of the island and surrounding reefs. Additional wilderness information and evaluation are covered in greater detail in Appendix F.

3.14 Archaeology and Paleontology

Environmental conditions at Jarvis are inhospitable to lengthy human occupation. A lack of a constant supply of fresh water is the primary limiting factor for habitation by humans. It is conceivable that early prehistoric people could have used Jarvis Island as a stopping, resting, or gathering place during their voyages across the Pacific Ocean, including capture of nesting sea turtles kept alive for extended food supply during long ocean voyages and the collection of seabirds. However, it is doubtful that voyagers would have willingly settled on this island. Landings in any vessel would have been difficult, although access gained by small canoe is possible. Due to Jarvis Island's remoteness and lack of a sustainable freshwater supply, it is likely that Jarvis Island played a minimal role, if any, in the colonizing efforts of prehistoric people across the Pacific. Although evidence exists of Polynesian occupancy in the Phoenix and Line Islands, data specific to Jarvis is lacking (Emory. 1939, Brown, et al. 2002).

No records were found of paleontological surveys, although paleontological resources could exist in the form of fossilized coral or algae and other invertebrates. The chances of prehistoric indigenous terrestrial mammals inhabiting Jarvis Island are non-existent due to the geological forces that formed the island, and its remoteness and dry climate.

3.15 Recent Cultural History

The occupation and use of Jarvis Island after post-European contact, approximately AD 1800, can be divided into four distinctive time periods or eras based upon alternating periods of occupation, use, and abandonment. The eras are categorized as whaling, guano mining, colonizing, and post military.

Whaling era 1800-1850
Use of the island by whaling ship crews is speculative. Lacking an adequate harbor or sheltered bay, landings on the island are difficult to this day. However, whaling vessels may have stopped at Jarvis Island to acquire birds, eggs, and turtles.

Jarvis Island was initially discovered and named by Captain Brown for the owner of the vessel *Eliza Francis* when he mapped it in 1821. The island has also been called Bunker, Volunteer, Brook, and Brock. Captain Michael Baker of the ship *Braganza* landed in 1835 and documented the rich guano deposits leading to the island later being claimed in 1857 by Alfred Benson and Charles Judd for the American Guano Company as authorized by the Guano Act of 1856.

Guano Mining Era: 1850-1891
On February 5, 1857, Alfred G. Benson and Charles H. Judd on board the Hawaiian schooner *Liholiho* officially claimed the island under the "Guano Act" of 1856 for the American Guano Company (Bryan 1974). Guano mining on Jarvis Island was started in 1858 and continued except for a cessation during the Civil War until little quality guano remained in 1879. At the termination of the lease approximately 300,000 tons of guano had been removed making it one of the richest deposits in the Central Pacific Ocean (Hutchinson, 1950). Evidence of this era of exploitation still remains as large basins from mining excavations and mounds of low-grade guano mark the island landscape.

In 1913 the barkentine *Amaranth* coming with a cargo of coal from New South Wales and heading for San Francisco hit the Southeast side of Jarvis Island. The Captain and crew took to their boats and landed the next morning. The vessel broke up. The crew had salvaged provisions and water from the Amaranth and managed to reach Samoa in the two boats 3 weeks later. The Whippoorwill Expedition sponsored by Bishop Museum paid a scientific visit in 1924. A memorial cairn and plaque commemorates the grounding and is still present on the island.

Colonizing Era: 1935-1942

The establishment of trans-Pacific air routes; territorial ownership disputes over several islands in the Pacific between the United States and the United Kingdom in the early 1900s; and the threat of a second world war led to colonizing efforts by the United States on several Pacific Islands including Jarvis Island. Colonizing efforts began in March 1935. Several military personnel and graduates of Kamehameha Schools, Hawaii established a colony on Jarvis Island (Brown et al. 2002). After initial establishment, the colonists were comprised of Kamehameha graduates and were supplied with enough food, water and other necessities to sustain them "for a period of from six weeks to several months" (Bryan 1974). Water and bulk food were supplied from Hawaii. During this colonizing era, at least 26 trips were made to Jarvis Island by various United States Coast Guard (USCG) cutters. During the colonizing era, Jarvis Island was visited frequently and was often the scene of busy activity.

Structures for water, food storage, radio equipment, and walls around the main settlement were constructed in part using lumber remaining from the wreck of the *Amaranth*. Attempts to grow trees, flowers, and vegetables were made, but the climate was unfavorable for cultivated crops.

Jarvis Island was evacuated at the beginning of World War II and remained unoccupied during the remainder of the war.

Post War Era: 1944 to present

No attempt was made to re-colonize Jarvis Island after the war, although the Department of the Interior thought of doing so. In 1948, the U.S. decided that the claim to Jarvis Island could be effectively maintained by annual USCG visits. Thus, a USCG vessel apparently first visited the island after the war. USCG vessels that visited Howland Island included the *Kettle*, *Basswood*, *Buttonwood*, *Kukui*, the *Planetree*, *Blackhaw* and *Ironwood*. Most visits to Jarvis usually occurred in the first 4 months of the year with the ships' crews completing repairs to the day beacon and taking photographs to establish their presence on the island.

In March 1963, and for the following 2 years, Smithsonian Institution employees made a number of visits to Jarvis Island as part of the POBSP (Clapp, 1967)

In recent years, sporadic visits have been made by Refuge Staff aboard USCG and NOAA vessels. The island and its territorial seas were transferred to the Service in 1974 from the Office of Insular Affairs. This area is now managed as a unit of the System. Refuge staff continue to participate in scientific expeditions, typically aboard NOAA vessels and occurring once every 2 years since 2000.

3.16 Socio-economics

Historical Developments

Since whaling days, Jarvis Island has been used for a variety of commercial enterprises. During the whaling era, Jarvis may have served as a gathering site for provisions by harvesting seabirds, sea turtles, and their eggs. Fishing for tuna and other species may also have occurred. The guano-mining era provided the world with a nutrient-rich fertilizer. Jarvis and other central Pacific islands were exploited for their rich guano deposits.

After the guano-mining period, Jarvis Island was retained by the U.S. Government, to aid in transportation and commerce during the mid-1930s. A colony was established on Jarvis Island to assert U.S. possession by placing 4 to 5 men on Jarvis Island from 1935 to 1942 (Bryan 1974, Brown et al. 2002 After 1945, USCG vessels performed annual patrols to protect U.S. economic interests in the central Pacific.

In 1974, Jarvis Island and its territorial sea was transferred to the Service as a unit of the System to preserve and restore ecosystem values, focusing on nesting seabird populations

During the past decade, the government of Kiribati requested permission to allow their fishing fleets within Jarvis Island's 200-mile Exclusive Economic Zone (EEZ). Subsequently, the Service working with the U.S. State Department have denied Kiribati's request. There are no current economic uses of Jarvis, and the island remains unpopulated.

Land Use
Jarvis Island has been uninhabited since the World War II era and will remain so except for occupation during periodic field camps. As such, the future "land use" for Jarvis Island will likely include designation of a preferred field campsite that will not conflict with important wildlife functions, habitat restoration, cultural sites, or wilderness values. Site planning will also identify corridors for small boat access, footpaths for regular island patrols, study sites, areas designated for solar power and potable water production generation, waste and trash disposal areas, work areas, and other needs.

Public Access
Howland is closed to public access. There has never been, nor are there plans to formally open the refuge to recreational activities by publishing public notice in the Federal Register. However, limited public access of Howland has been authorized in the past. Refuge access is managed through the issuance of a SUP when the activity is deemed compatible and appropriate with the purposes of refuge establishment.

Commercial Fishing
Over the years commercial fishing vessels may have targeted uninhabited Jarvis for unauthorized and illegal fishing because of the lack of on-site surveillance and enforcement capacity. Jarvis is habitat to many commercially valuable fishery species including sharks, lobsters, groupers, giant clams, tuna, wahoo, swordfish, deepwater snappers, bumphead parrotfish, humphead wrasses, various aquarium fish, pearl oysters, sea cucumbers, and other species. The no-take mandate and establishment of the refuge predated the applicability of the Magnuson-Stevens Fishery Conservation and Management Act of 1996 as amended (16 USC 1361 et seq.) to Jarvis. Neither the Western Pacific Regional Fishery Management Council (WESPAC) nor NOAA Fisheries advocates commercial fishing within Jarvis, although both share commercial fishery management responsibilities for waters outside the refuge boundaries. The deep slope area outside the refuge is likely too small to support commercial bottomfish harvest especially in light of the long commuting distances between Jarvis and the home ports of the fishing vessels. However, foreign fishing vessels may target Jarvis for illegal commercial fishery harvest, and the

economic pressure to pursue this option will likely increase in the future as commercial fishing stocks in Asia and the Pacific become more heavily fished and depleted.

This page left intentionally blank.

Chapter 4: Environmental Consequences

4.1 Introduction

All alternatives presented in this document describe varying levels of management activity on Jarvis. These range from establishing an overnight field camp once every two years and conducting basic biological surveys, to establishing a year-round field camp every five years, conducting additional biological and ecological surveys, and basic habitat management practices such as invasive species control. Other than infrequent field camps, Jarvis is unoccupied throughout the year. Permanent infrastructure development is not a component of any alternative. Field camps are temporary, mobile, and removed at the end of each field camp season. The few potential adverse impacts are generally temporary, localized, and can be fully mitigated or avoided. As a result, most of the impacts of all alternatives are beneficial and designed to maintain Jarvis in a natural wilderness state driven by natural process, and to restore native species and habitats that may have been lost in the past.

Alternatives primarily differ in their degree of affording staff visitation and surveillance of the refuge, which in turn have varying degrees of effectiveness on reducing alien and invasive species, unauthorized visitation and harvest, monitoring the status of fish and wildlife, and instituting restoration programs such as the reestablishment of extirpated nesting seabird species. All four alternatives would generally result in some positive impacts to the refuge. However, continuing the existing levels of visitation is not guaranteed and relies on partners being capable and willing to provide transportation for Service staff to Jarvis and other remote Pacific Island refuges. Should partner support curtail or cease, the present level of visitation would be substantially reduced or eliminated along with corresponding increases in adverse effects to refuge fish and wildlife.

The world today is a smaller and more crowded place. In the past Jarvis and several other remote Pacific Island refuges could "take care of themselves" without the need for human intervention. During many past centuries, they benefited from their marginal/inhospitable living conditions, small size, dangerous shore access, and isolation from human population settlements. However, this is no longer the case. During the past 2 centuries, all were visited and exploited for sea turtles and seabird guano, feathers, and eggs. This century found them modified in preparation for global conflict, and more recently disturbed by climate change, invasive species, poachers, anglers, adventurers, and other unauthorized visitors. The overriding management need for Jarvis, and the other Pacific Island refuges is to provide adequate staff visitation and surveillance to mitigate and protect the refuge from these and other forces.

Alternative A, the No Action alternative describes limited staff visits and management activity on Jarvis. Alternatives B, C and D provide strategies to increase management activities and use electronic and remote sensing equipment at the refuge to varying degrees. However, a substantial increase in internal Service funding (most likely from RONS) to implement either Alternative C or D would be required. These two alternatives (C, D) establish a temporary field camp lasting up to one year on Jarvis Island, which could result in disturbances to wildlife. However, all possible effects can be mitigated through advanced planning and scientific surveys.

Except for minor disturbance to possible historic sites that can be avoided or mitigated through archaeological and cultural surveys, and minor wildlife disturbance during seasonal field camp missions, none of the alternative actions themselves would result in adverse impacts and most all of the remaining effects are positive, although more so for Alternatives C or D. The following sections evaluate the consequences of implementing Alternatives A – D. Table 4.1 summarizes the similarities among and differences between alternatives.

4.2 Geology and Soils

The geology and soils of Jarvis and surrounding coral reefs likely would not be affected by any of the alternatives. Field camps, whether overnight, or year-round would consist of temporary shelters (tents) which rest on the surface of the soil, only penetrating where a tent stake has to be driven into the soil in order to stabilize the shelter. Archeological and cultural resource surveys, required of Alternatives C and D before establishment of field camps will disturb soil surface at the location of the survey. Since these surveys will be localized and completed by trained archeologist, impacts are thought to be minimal. Subsurface surveys will not be required for overnight field camps described in Alternatives A and B. The disturbance to soils from an overnight camp is thought to be minimal since soil texture is either coarse, being composed of sand, or already compacted and dense, being solidified by the soluble phosphates becoming fixed to the coral sand and limestone. Field camps and biological surveys have a risk of soil compaction along well traveled trails and at campsites. This risk is greater for Alternatives C and D due to the longer length of time that biologists would be present on the island. However, this risk is thought to not have a long term or detrimental impact to the soils or geology of Jarvis since the soils are either resistant to compaction or already naturally compacted.

4.3 Air and Water Quality

4.3.1 Air Quality

None of alternatives (A-D) likely would have any measurable or long-term impact on air quality. Air quality over the ocean and on the island is pristine, and none of the alternatives would affect the pristine atmospheric character of Jarvis.

Indirectly, ship traffic to and from Jarvis would generate some noise and exhaust emissions. On average across all alternatives during the life of this plan, transport vessels would generally operate in nearshore waters approximately 2 days per year. Small boats operating during field camp deployment and demobilization would use modern four-stroke outboard engines that emit low noise and exhaust levels. Overall effects to air quality would be minimal and temporary. Field camps and transport vessels also have the capability to produce unnatural lighting at night, which could disturb some light sensitive bird species, such as petrels and boobies, and detract from the visual clarity of night skies. These effects will be avoided or minimized by establishing night-time operating procedures for ships and field camps that limit the amount of light, and require window shades to block interior lights.

4.3.2 Water Quality and Ocean Environment

Marine water quality as well as ambient currents, swells, waves, and tidal fluctuations likely would not be affected by actions associated with any of the alternatives. No physical modification of the shoreline is proposed as part of any alternative. To the contrary, more frequent marine debris and shoreline flotsam collections during field camp operations for Alternatives C and D would result in modest beneficial effects to coastal and marine environments.

A policy of 'pack it in, pack it out' will be standard for all alternatives, thus there will be no impact to water quality and the ocean environment. This policy will also apply to human excrement. Biodegradable (composting) toilets, sealable chemical toilets, or simply sealable containers (double bagged zip-lock bags) used to contain human waste will eliminate any potential negative impacts. All trash and waste will be removed during field camp demobilization.

4.4 Biological Resources

4.4.1 Terrestrial Habitats and Wildlife

General
All alternatives impacts would have benefits to terrestrial and marine wildlife including vegetation, insects, crabs, insects, reptiles, seabirds, shorebirds, fish, and corals. However, Alternatives C and D would result in comparatively more benefits than Alternatives A and B. Alternative B would be similar in scope to Alternative A, but occur more frequently. More frequent and thorough staff visits would improve detection rates of, and response to invasive plants and animals. All alternatives propose to re-establish breeding populations of two rare petrel species. Remote sensing capacity under Alternatives C and D would allow rapid detection of unauthorized trespassers and discourage others from visiting Jarvis without proper and prior permission from the Service. In turn, these added capabilities would reduce the threat of invasive species introductions via the clothing, shoes, supplies, and vessels of possible trespassers.

Two of the alternatives (C and D) would increase the human presence on and management of Jarvis, especially the terrestrial environment. Wildlife disturbance would increase as staff and scientists move about on patrols, conduct research, remove possible invasive species, erect tents and other camp facilities, gather and dispose of waste, collect accumulated floating and emergent marine debris, and restore some habitats. These activities would be scheduled and located on the island where disturbance would be temporary and localized. Even under any possible scenario, the degree of detrimental effects would be minor and outweighed by the benefits of having a fully functional field camp on the island.

Habitat
There will be minor and temporary disturbance to terrestrial habitats under all alternatives. All field camps, regardless of duration, will create a 'footprint', or disturbed area surrounding the

camping and cooking area. Impacts may be trampling of vegetation or covering vegetation with tents or tarps. These impacts can be reduced or eliminated by selecting field camp sites with limited or no vegetation. Since there will be little to no soil surface disturbance, vegetation will fully recover once field camp is demobilized.

The footprint of the field camp described in Alternative A and B has less chance of impacting habitat due to the shorter time period that biologist would be on-site.

Seabirds

Alternatives A and B would have a temporary (1 to 2 day per year or every other year) disturbance to nesting seabirds due to biologists conducting surveys and establishing a field camp. These disturbances will be minimized by locating field camps away from nesting colonies, and only approaching nesting colonies to collect scientific data such as species presence, population numbers, and nesting activity. Alternatives C and D, seasonal and year-long field camps respectively would have increasingly more potential disturbance simply from staff being present on the island. However, these disturbances will be minimized in the same manner as for Alternatives A and B. The additional survey components of Alternatives C and D of nesting success and nesting chronology will require biologists to enter the seabird breeding colony. Precautions such as limited time spent in the colony, and collecting/observing a representative sample instead of the entire colony will limit disturbances. Under all alternatives, these minor disturbances are temporary in nature and will not affect Jarvis's resources once the field camps are demobilized.

Seabird nest attraction devices, if successful in attracting Phoenix petrel and Polynesian storm-petrel to Jarvis, will provide these populations with an additional nesting location that is free from mammalian predators. It is difficult to predict the overall impact that reestablishment of nesting by these species on Jarvis will have on their overall population status. However, since predator-free islands in the Pacific are rare, predator-free islands such as Howland are becoming more important to ground nesting seabird species such as the Phoenix petrel and Polynesian storm-petrel.

Shorebirds

All alternatives will have minimal impact to shorebird resources. Biological surveys and field campsites have the potential to displace or disturb shorebird loafing and foraging sites. However, the relative impact of human activity and imprint of the field camp to areas that shorebirds utilize is minimal.

Reptiles

Management activities such as biological surveys and campsites described in all the alternatives will have minimal impact to reptile resources since the estimated area of the field camp and survey routes (approximately 1 acre) is a minor percent (approximately 0.0015%) of the overall habitat available to reptiles on the island. While biological surveys and campsites have the potential to displace or disturb reptiles, there are ample other areas of suitable habitat.

Invertebrates

Management activities such as biological surveys and campsites described in all the alternatives will have minimal impact to the land invertebrates resources, specifically land hermit crabs, since the estimated area of the field camp and survey routes (approximately 1 acre) is a minor percent (approximately 0.0015%) of the overall habitat available to land hermit crabs on the island. While biological surveys and field camp sites have the potential to displace or disturb invertebrates, there are ample other areas of suitable habitat.

4.4.2 Marine Habitats, Fish, and Wildlife

General

Marine fish, wildlife, and submergent habitats would not be adversely affected by any of the alternatives. The increased on-site visitation proposed for Alternatives B, C, and D would discourage poaching and unauthorized harvest of sharks, giant clams, other reef fish, corals and other invertebrates, sea turtles, and other species used in the aquarium trade. All alternatives would maintain Jarvis as closed to recreational and commercial fishing and harvesting, except for those activities authorized by SUP. Greater presence and enhanced monitoring of selected marine species during field camp operations would result in better understanding and protection of corals and other key marine species. Enhanced marine assessment and monitoring would also allow early detection and control of marine invasive species. Therefore, the net result of the proposed action would be slightly beneficial for marine fish and wildlife while the other action alternatives would have greater benefit.

Corals

All alternatives have potential to disturb corals during field camp deployment and demobilization. Small boat operations will necessarily cross shallow water reef areas to reach the shoreline of the island. During periods of calm seas, natural and manmade cuts in the reef allow safe passage of small boats. However, the potential exists for strong currents, surf, or wind to push boats onto the reef. Boats will not be allowed to land on the island during unsafe conditions, thereby limiting the threat of reef damage. Anchorage of transport vessel also poses a threat to corals. To the extent possible, transport vessels are requested not to anchor, but rather stay stationary during deployment and demobilization. If anchoring is required, anchors will be placed in deep water areas devoid of coral cover. Thus, impacts to coral are expected to be minimal.

Marine surveys also have the potential to disturb corals. Inattentive snorkel and SCUBA activities have the risk of equipment contacting coral. Alternatives C and D, with their increased marine surveys have a greater risk than Alternatives A and B. However, this threat is minimal since trained scientists will conduct all marine surveys.

Fish

All alternatives will have minimal opportunity to impact fish resources. Recreational, sustenance, and commercial fishing activity is prohibited on the refuge, and will continue to be prohibited across all alternatives.

Marine Mammals

Marine mammals are found in the nearshore waters of Jarvis. Encounters with vessels are only possible during transport to island or conduct of marine surveys. While this threat increases for Alternatives C and D, this threat is minimal due to the very limited amount of time vessels would have the opportunity to disturb marine mammals. Having full-time access to a vessel, as described in Alternative D would provide the opportunity to conduct specific surveys for marine mammals and would add to the baseline of scientific information on their use of Jarvis. All other alternatives utilize vessels strictly for transport and do not appreciably add to our baseline of scientific information.

Marine Turtles

Impacts to marine turtles are reported in the following section, 4.4.3 Threatened and Endangered Species.

4.4.3 Threatened and Endangered Species

The threatened green sea turtle and endangered hawksbill sea turtle will not be impacted by any of the proposed alternatives. During the infrequent visits to Jarvis, these species may encounter small boats during field camp deployment and demobilization, or larger vessels during arrivals and departures. The probability of a sea turtle being struck by a boat during these infrequent events, roughly twice per year, is very low. Small boat operations will be limited to minimum safe operating speeds to minimize any risk that may exist. There would be no effect to sea turtles caused by monitoring activities on the island. Any turtles found to be loafing on exposed shoreline are easily avoided. Those seen during marine surveys are equally easy to avoid. Alternatives A and B provide limited opportunity to improve our understanding of the turtles habitat use. The short length of time of these field camps allow for only casual observations of turtles. Longer term field camps described in Alternatives C and D would provide more opportunity for observing turtles. Additionally, full time access to a vessel as described in Alternative D would increase the opportunity to survey for turtles. Even so, the anticipated amount of survey data would not considerably increase our knowledge base of turtle use of Jarvis. No specific surveys are planned. Remote sensing and/or the physical presence of the field camp would help to discourage any potential illegal take. Unauthorized harvest would especially be unlikely during the 1-year-long field camp established every third year at Jarvis under Alternative D. None of the actions described in any of these alternatives will have impacts to the two listed turtle species. Therefore, formal consultation with NOAA-NMFS, in accordance with section 7 of the Endangered Species Act of 1973 is not required and will not be initiated.

4.5 Wilderness Resources

The wilderness values of Jarvis would not be adversely affected by any of the alternatives. No permanent structures, roads, or other features would be constructed. The proposed field camp under all alternatives would be temporary, dismantled, and removed after each field camp. This temporary field camp and the activities associated with its operation would be considered the "minimum tool", as defined in the Draft Wilderness Stewardship Policy pursuant to the

Wilderness Act of 1964 (66 FR 3708). Alternatives C or D may also improve the wilderness character of the island by removing abandoned batteries and other unsightly debris

4.6 Cultural Resources

Cultural resources at Jarvis may include archaeological and historic sites. The Jarvis Light day beacon, *Amaranth* memorial, guano mining borrow pits, and ruins of colonization era occupations are apparent on the surface but many of the archaeological sites may be subsurface or in the marine environment and not apparent except to trained archeologists. Deployment of field camps has limited potential to impact subsurface archeological or historical resources. Alternatives A and B would have the least potential to disturb archeological or cultural resources due to the limited staff time on-island and transient nature of the field camps. Prior to establishment of field camps for Alternative C or Alternative D, archaeological reconnaissance surveys with limited sub-surface testing will be used to identify the precise locations of all sites and afford preliminary assessment of their nature, function, and significance of any cultural sites. Field campsites would be situated to avoid affecting any identified sites. Consequently all alternatives would have minimal long-term effects. Other management activities such as biological surveys, invasive species control, or marine debris collection and removal would likewise have limited potential to impact cultural resources. In this manner, impacts to cultural resources would be very unlikely for Alternatives A and B, and minor and avoidable for Alternatives C and D. Under Alternatives C and D, only trained archeologists will complete archeological and cultural surveys. Surveys will only be used to document the presence or absence of artifacts.

4.7 Economic Effects

Jarvis is currently managed with a portion of several Remotes employees staff time. Taken collectively under Alternative A, staff time devoted to Jarvis is approximately 1/5 of one permanent positions salary in a given year. Alternative B increases this amount to approximately 1/3 of a permanent positions annual salary. Implementing Alternatives C and D would increase the staffing needs by approximately two additional annual permanent salaries. None of the positions or portions of positions, beyond the current 1/5 of one salary is funded. It would be possible to adjust position duties of existing staff to cover the increase needed to implement Alternative B. Additional funding would be required to implement Alternatives C or D.

4.8 Environmental Justice

Executive Order 12898 requires all federal agencies to address and identify, as appropriate, disproportionately high and adverse human health or environmental effects of its programs, policies, and activities on minority populations, low-income populations, and Indian Tribes in the United States. There are no populations, minority, low-income, or otherwise, in the vicinity of Jarvis. The nearest inhabited land mass to Jarvis is Kiritimati Island, 184 nmi to the north. The nearest inhabited U.S. landmass is Hawaii at 1,263 nmi. Due to the extensive distances between human populations and Jarvis, no adverse human health or environmental effects were identified for minority or low-income populations, Indian Tribes, or anyone else.

4.9 Cumulative Effects

Overall, there are minimal long-term adverse impacts to the terrestrial or marine resources of Jarvis. Vegetation trampled during field camp operations will fully recover during subsequent seasons when field camps are not present. Precautions will limit disturbance to seabird colonies. There will be no permanent facilities or survey markers erected. All trash will be collected and removed from the island at the end of all field camp seasons. Aside from the potential establishment of nesting seabird species, there will be no physical sign that any of these alternatives has been implemented. The only other beneficial affects or impacts will be knowledge based through the collection and dissemination of scientific information. Considered in their totality, the adverse or beneficial impacts of any alternative to the physical, observable resources of Jarvis will not be noticeable and thus insignificant.

Table 4.1 Summary of Effects under CCP Alternatives

	Alternative A	Alternative B	Alternative C	Alternative D
Physical Environment Effects				
Geology and Soils	Neutral effect. Coarse soils and infrequent site visits preclude effects of trampling or disturbance.	Neutral effect. Although frequency of site visits increases, the level of visitation still precludes the effects of trampling or disturbance.	Minor but temporary negative effect due to soil compaction and disturbance along established trails.	Minor but temporary negative effect due to soil compaction and disturbance along established trails.
Air and Water Quality	Minor but temporary negative effect from noise and exhaust emission of transport and local boat traffic.	Minor but temporary negative effect from noise and exhaust emission of transport and local boat traffic.	Slight negative effect due to field camp operations and limited use of gas-powered generator. Minor but temporary negative effect from transport and local boat traffic remain constant with other alternatives.	Slight negative effect due to field camp operations and limited use of gas-powered generator increases slightly over Alternative C. Minor but temporary negative effect from transport and local boat traffic remain constant with other alternatives.
Environmental Contaminants	Neutral effect. No known existing contaminants, although potential exists for fuel spills during deployment and demobilization of field camp.	Neutral effect. No known existing contaminants, although potential exists for fuel spills during deployment and demobilization of field camp.	Neutral effect. No known existing contaminants, although potential increases slightly for fuel spills during deployment, operation, and demobilization of field camp.	Neutral effect. No known existing contaminants, although potential increases slightly for fuel spills during deployment, operation, and demobilization of field camp.

	Alternative A	Alternative B	Alternative C	Alternative D
Effects to Wildlife and Habitat				
Terrestrial Habitats	Neutral to slightly positive effect. Habitat management limited to stockpile marine debris.	Neutral to slightly positive effect. Habitat management limited to stockpile marine debris.	Moderately positive effect. Habitat management includes stockpile and removal of marine debris.	Moderately positive effect. Habitat management includes stockpile and removal of marine debris.
Invasive Species	Neutral effect. Invasive species documentation occurs during course of other duties. Potential negative effect exists for invasive species to become established during two-year staff absence between visits.	Neutral effect. Invasive species documentation occurs during course of other duties. Potential negative effect reduced for invasive species to become established during one- year staff absence between visits.	Moderately positive effect. Surveys and control activities of invasive species occur annually during the 4-month field camp.	Slightly positive effect. Surveys and control activities of invasive species occur every 5th year. Duration of field camp (12-month) compensates for lengthened time between field camps.
Seabirds	Neutral effect. Basic monitoring of species presence/absence occurs every other year.	Slightly positive effect. Basic monitoring of species presence/absence occurs every year. Electronic calls have potential positive effect to restore 2 nesting seabird species.	Moderate positive effect. Expanded monitoring activities increase scientific understanding of seabird biology. Electronic calls have potential positive effect to restore 2 nesting seabird species.	Moderate positive effect. Expanded monitoring activities increase scientific understanding of seabird biology. Electronic calls have potential positive effect to restore 2 nesting seabird species.
Shorebirds	Neutral effect. No change from current condition.	Neutral effect. No change from current condition.	Neutral effect. No change from current condition.	Neutral effect. No change from current condition.
Other Wildlife	Neutral effect. No change from current condition.	Neutral effect. No change from current condition.	Neutral effect. No change from current condition.	Neutral effect. No change from current condition.

	Alternative A	Alternative B	Alternative C	Alternative D
Marine Habitats	Neutral effect. No change from current condition.	Neutral to minor positive effect. Potential positive effect of deep water surveys to increase understanding of marine ecosystem.	Neutral to minor positive effect. Potential positive effect of deep water surveys to increase understanding of marine ecosystem.	Neutral to minor positive effect. Potential positive effect of deep water surveys to increase understanding of marine ecosystem.
Corals	Potential slight negative effect by grounding during deployment and demobilization of field camps. Standardized surveys conducted.	Potential slight negative effect by grounding during deployment and demobilization of field camps. Standardized surveys conducted.	Potential slight negative effect by grounding during deployment and demobilization of field camps. Positive effect of increased surveys to increase understanding of corals, but potential slight negative effect from observer disturbance/damage to corals.	Potential slight negative effect by grounding during deployment and demobilization of field camps. Positive effect of increased surveys to increase understanding of corals, but potential slight negative effect from observer disturbance/damage to corals.
Fish	Neutral effect. No change from current condition.	Neutral effect. No change from current condition.	Neutral effect. No change from current condition.	Neutral effect. No change from current condition.
Marine Mammals	Neutral effect. No change from current condition.	Neutral effect. No change from current condition.	Neutral effect. No change from current condition	Moderate positive effect. Full time access to vessel allows for additional surveys.
Threatened and Endangered Species	Neutral effect. No change from current condition.	Neutral effect. No change from current condition	Slight positive effect. Increased opportunity to survey.	Moderate positive effect. Increased opportunity to survey.

	Alternative A	Alternative B	Alternative C	Alternative D
Social and Other Effects				
Wilderness Resources	Neutral effect. No change from current condition. Wilderness values exist, but no wilderness designation.	Neutral effect. Wilderness Study Areas identified for both terrestrial and marine areas of refuge.	Neutral effect. Wilderness Study Areas identified for both terrestrial and marine areas of refuge.	Neutral effect. Wilderness Study Areas identified for both terrestrial and marine areas of refuge.
Historic and Cultural Resources	Neutral effect. No change from current condition.	Neutral effect. No change from current condition.	Minor positive effect. Cultural resource survey required prior to field camp establishment. Maintenance of historical structures possible.	Minor positive. Cultural resource survey required prior to field camp establishment. Maintenance of historical structures possible.
Socio-Economic	Neutral effect. No change from current condition.	Neutral to slight positive effect due to increased operational expenditures.	Moderate positive effect due to increased operational expenditures.	Moderate positive effect due to increased operational expenditures.
Environmental Justice	Neutral effect.	Neutral effect.	Neutral effect.	Neutral effect.
Cumulative Effects	Neutral effect.	Slight positive effect. Scale and scope of most management activities do not change from Alternative A.	Moderate positive effect. Greater scientific understanding of marine and terrestrial ecosystems is achieved. No long-term changes in habitat occur.	Moderate positive effect. Greater scientific understanding of marine and terrestrial ecosystems is achieved. No long-term changes in habitat occur.

Chapter 5: Consultation and Coordination with Others

5.1 Consultation and Coordination with Others

This section describes consultation and coordination efforts with the public, interested groups, and other agencies.

Planning Updates
The first Planning Update was mailed to 249 private individuals; nongovernmental organizations; local, state, Federal and international governments; and members of the media throughout the Pacific on October 12, 2005. This update announced the intent of the Service to produce a CCP for Jarvis, and invited comments on issues and concerns and interest in attending public meetings. A total of five responses were received.

A second planning update was mailed on May 17, 2006. This update announced the development of a list of alternatives and solicited comments on the draft alternatives. This update was mailed to 253 private individuals; non-governmental organizations; local, state, Federal and international governments; and members of the media throughout the Pacific. To date, no responses have been received.

Agency and Interest Group Consultation/Coordination
Members of the planning team met with NOAA staff and the Hawaii Department of Land and Natural Resources (DLNR) on May 31, 2005. Refuge staff also met with members of The Nature Conservancy on June 2, 2005. This second meeting introduced and offered the opportunity to be part of the planning process. Both NOAA and DLNR informally indicated that they were interested in the process, wished to be kept informed of planning progress and would review the draft plan when it became available.

A second meeting between State, NOAA, and Service staff was held on May 19, 2006 to discuss issues of mutual interest, which included their potential involvement in the Service's CCP process. A follow-up formal request was sent to the agencies on June 7, 2006. To date, neither DLNR nor NOAA has formally responded.

Federal Register Notices
The Notice of Intent to prepare a CCP for these refuges was published in the Federal Register on September 14, 2005. Public involvement was sought throughout the planning process using meetings, newsletters, and other communication tools.

Jarvis Island is uninhabited and an unincorporated U.S. territory far removed and beyond the jurisdiction of any State, insular area, or foreign nation. Other parties involved in correspondence related to this document included multiple nongovernmental organizations, U.S. Environmental Protection Agency; National Park Service; U.S. Geological Survey; U.S. Department of Defense; President's Advisory Council on Historic Preservation; National Oceanic and Atmospheric Administration (NOAA); Western Pacific Regional Fishery Management Council; Hawaii Department of Land and Natural Resources; Hawaii Office of

Hawaiian Affairs; Governor of Hawaii; the Honorary Consulate-General of the Republic of Kiribati; and the United Nations Educational, Scientific and Cultural Organization (UNESCO).

Appendix A

Glossary of Terms and Acronyms

ACHP. President's Advisory Council on Historic Preservation.

Alien species. Non-native species intentionally or accidentally introduced into habitats of the refuge.

Atoll. A tropical reef formation with a shallow water lagoon, surrounding perimeter reef, and reef islet(s).

Baker. Used alone in this report, it refers to the Baker Island National Wildlife Refuge.

CCP. Comprehensive Conservation Plan.

CCP/EA. A document that combines a Comprehensive Conservation Plan and an Environmental Assessment.

CFR. Code of Federal Regulations. A comprehensive directory of all Federal regulations.

CITES. Convention on the International Trade in Endangered Species of Wild Fauna and Flora.

Comprehensive Conservation Plan. A document that describes the desired future conditions of the refuge, and provides long-range guidance and management direction for the refuge manager to accomplish the purposes of the refuge, contribute to the mission of the System, and to meet other relevant mandates (Service Manual 602 FW 1.5).

CPWHP. Central Pacific World Heritage Project.

CRED. The Coral Reef Ecosystem Division of NOAA's Pacific Islands Fisheries Science Center.

DLNR. Hawaii Department of Land and Natural Resources.

DMA. Defense Mapping Agency.

EEZ. Exclusive Economic Zone.

EIS. Environmental Impact Statement. NEPA documentation that assesses the impacts of major Federal actions significantly affecting the quality of the human environment.

Environmental Assessment. A concise public document, prepared in compliance with the National Environmental Policy Act, that briefly discusses the purpose and need for an action, alternatives to such action, and provides sufficient evidence and analysis of impacts to determine whether to prepare an environmental impact statement or finding of no significant impact (40 CFR 1508.9).

ENSO. El Niño Southern Oscillation; a periodic ocean warming anomaly in the tropics.

EUC. Equatorial Undercurrent; a subsurface ocean current flowing east at the Equator.

Federal Register (FR). Official bulletin publicizing notices of Federal actions.

FMPS. Fishery Management Plans for commercial fisheries in Federal waters.

FONSI. Finding of No Significant Impact; a federal agency notice and preliminary decision that its proposed action would not require preparation of an EIS.

GIS. Geographic information system; a database integrating tabular and geographic data.

GPS. Global Positioning System; satellite-based for accurate geographic/site positioning.

Howland. Used alone in this report, it refers to the Howland Island National Wildlife Refuge.

Hydrophone. Underwater microphone or listening device.

Improvement Act. The National Wildlife Refuge System Improvement Act of 1997 amendment to the National Wildlife Refuge System Administration Act of 1966.

Insular Area. The current generic term used to refer to a United States possession, territory, Territory, freely associated state, or commonwealth under United States sovereignty.

Invasive Species. Either an alien or native species that spreads, or achieves dominance quickly, resulting in undesirable effects on native species and their habitats

ITCZ. Inter-tropical Convergence Zone; approximately along 5° N Latitude where the northeast and southeast tradewinds collide, rise, and create a zone of heavy rainfall and low winds; also known as the doldrums.

IUCN. International Union for the Conservation of Nature.

Jarvis. Used alone in this report, it refers to the Jarvis Island National Wildlife Refuge.

LEIS. Legislative Environmental Impact Statement. See EIS.

MBTA. Migratory Bird Treaty Act.

Mesoscale Eddy. A circular flow of water near an island or reef, roughly 10 to 100 nm in diameter caused by the wake of currents passing the reef or island.

µ L. Micro liter, or one-millionth of a liter.

NEC. North Equatorial Current, west-flowing surface current between 5-30°N Latitude.

NECC. North Equatorial Countercurrent; east-flowing surface current under the ITCZ.

NEPA. National Environmental Policy Act; establishes procedures requiring all Federal agencies to assess the environmental consequences of their actions.

NMI. Nautical mile; the equivalent of 1.15 statute (land) mile.

NMFS. The National Marine Fisheries Service of NOAA.

NOAA. National Oceanic and Atmospheric Administration.

NPS. National Park Service.

NWR. National Wildlife Refuge.

NWRS. National Wildlife Refuge System.

Oligotrophic. Waters having low levels of the mineral nutrients required by green plants. At Howland, this refers to the transparent zone of nutrient-poor shallow tropical waters, bounded by a thermocline serving as a barrier against exchange with deeper nutrient-rich waters.

Phenology. The study of periodic biological phenomena, such as breeding, flowering, and migrations, especially as related to climate.

Preferred Alternative. This is the alternative determined [by the decision maker] to best achieve the refuge purpose(s), vision, and goals; contributes to the Refuge System mission, addresses the issues; and is consistent with principles of sound fish and wildlife management.

Proposed Action. Preferred Alternative among several evaluated to comply with NEPA.

Quadrat. A rigid frame used by ecologists to facilitate unit area estimates of the size and density of surface-dwelling plants and animals; **Photo-quadrat.** A photograph of the area inside the quadrat to allow office data analysis after field staff visits.

PIFSC. NOAA's Pacific Islands Fisheries Science Center.

REA. Rapid ecological assessments.

Reef Island. Low tropical islet resting on a coral reef and consisting of reef rock and sand.

RONS. Refuge Operating Needs System; Service program for NWR operating funds.

ROV. Remotely operated vehicle; mobile un-manned device for collecting deep-sea data.

SAMMS. Service Asset Maintenance Management System; Service program to provide funds to maintain refuge property.

SEC. South Equatorial Current; westward-flowing ocean current driven by the southeast tradewinds between Latitudes 5° N and 30° S.

Secretary. The Secretary of the Interior.

Service. Used alone in this report, it refers to the U. S. Fish and Wildlife Service.

SIPOBS. Smithsonian Institution Pacific Ocean Biological Survey.

SUP. Special Use Permit; written Service approval and conditions for conducting an activity in a refuge.

System. Used alone in this report, it refers to the National Wildlife Refuge System.

Thermocline. In oceans, it is a depth zone of rapid density and temperature change serving as a barrier between mixing of shallow warmer surface and deeper subsurface waters.

Transect. A linear scientific field survey sampling design or area to facilitate repeatability, standard units of measurement, and future site relocation and resurvey.

UNESCO. United Nations Educational, Scientific and Cultural Organization.

USCG. United States Coast Guard.

U.S. Possession. Equivalent to *U.S. territory*. It is no longer current colloquial usage.

U.S. Territory. An incorporated United States insular area, of which only one currently exists, Palmyra Atoll, in which the United States Congress has applied the full body of the United States Constitution.

U.S. territory. A United States insular area in which the United States Congress has determined that only selected parts of the United States Constitution apply.

WESPAC. Western Pacific Regional Fisheries Management Council.

WSA. Wilderness Study Area.

World Heritage Property. A protected and inscribed natural and/or cultural site with "outstanding universal value" and meeting one or more of the eligibility criteria of the International Convention on World Heritage.

Appendix B

Species Lists of Corals, Fish, Vegetation and Birds

Table B-1: Coral species and genera reported at Jarvis Island National Wildlife Refuge during surveys in 2000, 2001, 2002, 2004 and 2006. Asterisks (*) identify soft corals (Order Alcyonaria), and two asterisks (**) identify Class Hydrozoa stony corals. All others are stony corals from the Order Scleractinia. (After Maragos unpublished)

Scientific Name	Scientific Name
CLASS HYDROZOA	**AGARICIIDAE**
Stylaster sp.**	*Pavona maldivensis*
*Distichopora violacea***	*Leptoseris mycetoseroides*
MILLEPORIDAE	*Pachyseris* sp.
Millepora platyphylla	*Pavona explanulata*
POCILLOPORIDAE	*Pavona minuta*
Pocillopora eydouxi	*Pavona varians*
Pocillopora meandrina	*Pavona clavus*
Pocillopora verrucosa	**FUNGIIDAE**
Pocillopora brevicornis	*Fungia scutaria*
Pocillopora zelli	*Fungia granulose*
ACROPORIDAE	**MERULINIDAE**
Montipora caliculata	*Hydnophora microconos*
Montipora tuberculosa	**FAVIIDAE**
Montipora aequituberculata	*Favites pentagona*
Montipora efflorescens	*Favites rotumana*
Montipora informis	*Goniastrea retiformis*
Montipora monasteriata	*Favia matthaii*
Montipora verrilli	*Favia stelligera*
Acropora abrotanoides	**SIDERASTREIDAE**
Acropora tutuilensis	*Psammocora nierstraszi*
Acropora cytherea	*Psammocora cf. verrilli*
Acropora nana	*Psammocora haimeana*
Acropora spicifera	*Cladopsammia* sp.
Acropora subulata	*Coscinaraea* sp.
Acropora verweyi	*Echinophyllia aspera*
PORITIDAE	**ORDER ALCYONARIA**
Porites australiensis	*Lobophytum* sp.*
Porites lobata	*Sinularia* sp.*
Porites vaughani	
Porites solida	

Table B-2: Fish species and genera reported at Jarvis Island National Wildlife Refuge, after unpublished records compiled by Bruce C. Mundy, Richard Wass, Edward DeMartini, Brian Greene, Brian Zgliczynski, and Robert E. Schroeder (2002).

Scientific Name	Common Name
CARCHARHINIDAE	**Requiem Sharks**
Carcharhinus amblyrhynchos (Bleeker, 1856)	grey reef shark
Carcharhinus melanopterus (Quoy &Gaimard, 1824)	reef black-tip shark
Carcharhinus albimarginatus (Rüppell, 1837)	silvertip shark
HEMIGALEIDAE	**Weasel Sharks, White-tip Reef Sharks**
Triaenodon obesus (Rüppell, 1837)	white-tip reef shark
SPHYRNIDAE	**Hammerhead Sharks**
Sphyrna lewini (Griffith & Smith, 1834)	scalloped hammerhead shark
Sphyrna mokarran (Rüppell, 1837)	great hammerhead shark
Sphyrna sp.	unidentified *Sphyrna* species
DASYATIDAE	**Sand Rays**
Taeniura meyeni (Müller & Henle, 1841)	giant sand ray
MYLIOBATIDAE	**Eagle Rays**
Manta sp.	unidentified *Manta* species
MURAENIDAE	**Moray Eels**
Echidna nebulosa (Ahl, 1789)	snowflake moray
Echidna sp.	unidentified *Echidna* species
Enchelynassa canina (Quoy & Gaimard, 1824)	viper moray
Enchelycore pardalis (Temminck & Schlegel,1846)	moray eel
Gymnomuraena zebra (Shaw *in* Shaw & Nodder, 1797)	zebra moray
Gymnothorax breedini (McCosker & Randall, 1977)	Breeden's moray
Gymnothorax javanicus (Bleeker, 1859)	giant moray
Gymnothorax flavimarginatus (Rüppell, 1830)	yellow-margined moray
Gymnothorax meleagris (Shaw *in* Shaw & Nodder, 1795)	white-mouth moray
Gymnothorax monostigmus (Regan, 1909)	one-spot moray
Gymnothorax picta (Ahl, 1789)	peppered moray
Gymnothorax rueppelliae (McClelland, 1844)	yellow-headed moray
Gymnothorax sp.	unidentified *Gymnothorax* species.
Uropterygius concolor (Rüppell, 1838)	unicolor snake moray
Uropterygius xanthopterus (Bleeker, 1859)	yellow-fin snake moray

Scientific Name	Common Name
Uropterygius sp.	unidentified *Uropterygius* species
SYNODONTIDAE	**Lizardfishes**
Synodus sp.	unidentified *Synodus* species
HOLOCENTRIDAE	**Squirrelfishes and Soldierfishes**
Myripristis berndti (Jordan & Evermann, 1903)	bigscale soldierfish
Myripristis murdjan (Forsskål, 1775)	soldierfish
Sargocentron caudimaculatum (Rüppell, 1838)	tailspot squirrelfish
Sargocentron spiniferum (Forsskål, 1775)	long-jawed squirrelfish
Sargocentrum tiere (Cuvier in Cuvier & Valenciennes, 1829)	blue-lined squirrelfish
SCORPAENIDAE	**Scorpionfishes**
Scorpaenidae sp.	unidentified Scorpaenidae species (recorded by James Maragos)
Dendrochirus biocellatus (Fowler, 1938)	oscillated lionfish
Scorpaenopsis sp.	unidentified *Scorpaenopsis* species [perhaps *S. papuensis* (Cuvier *in* Cuvier & Valenciennes, 1829)]
Scorpaenopsis diabolis (Cuvier, 1829)	devil scorpionfish
Sebastapistes cyanostigma (Bleeker, 1856)	yellow-spotted scorpionfish
Sebastapistes mauritiana (Cuvier in Cuvier & Valenciennes 1829)	Mauritius scorpionfish
CARACANTHIDAE	**Orbicular Velvetfishes**
Caracanthus maculates (Gray, 1831)	spotted coral croucher
SERRANIDAE	**Sea Basses, Fairy Basslets & Groupers**
Cephalopholis argus (Bloch & Schneider, 1801)	peacock grouper
Cephalopholis leopardus (Lacepède, 1801)	leopard grouper
Cephalopholis miniatatus (Forsskål, 1775)	coral grouper
Cephalopholis urodeta (Forster *in* Bloch & Schneider, 1801)	flagtail grouper
Epinephelus fasciatus (Forsskål, 1775)	black-tipped grouper
Epinephelus hexagonatus (Forster in Bloch & Schneider, 1801)	hexagon grouper
Epinephelus howlandi (Günther, 1873)	Howland Island grouper
Epinephelus macrospilos (Bleeker, 1855)	black-spotted grouper
Epinephelus melanostigmus (Schultz in Schultz et al., 1953)	blackspot honeycomb grouper
Epinephelus merra (Bloch, 1793)	honeycomb grouper
Epinephelus retouti (Bleeker, 1868)	grouper
Epinephelus socialis (Günther, 1873)	tidepool grouper

Scientific Name	Common Name
Epinephelus spilotoceps (Schultz in Schultz et al., 1953)	four-saddle grouper
Epinephelus tauvina (Forsskål, 1775)	greasy grouper
Gracila albomarginata (Fowler & Bean, 1930)	white-margined grouper
Luzonichthys whitleyi (Smith, 1955)	Whitley's slender basslet
Pogonoperca punctata (Valenciennes *in* Cuvier & Valenciennes, 1830)	spotted soapfish
Pseudanthias bartlettorum (Randall & Lubbock, 1981)	Bartlett's fairy basslet
Pseudanthias bartlettorum var. "red spot" (Randall & Lubbock, 1981)	Bartlett's "red spot" basslet
Pseudanthias olivaceus (Randall & McCosker, 1982)	fairy basslet
Pseudantias sp.	unknown *Pseudantias* sp.
Variola louti (Forsskål, 1775)	lyretail grouper
PSEUDOCHROMIDAE	**Dottybacks**
Pseudochromidae sp.	unidentified Pseudochromidae species
BELONIDAE	**Needlefishes**
Tylosurus crocodilus (Peron & Lesueur in Lesueur, 1821)	crocodile needlefish
EXOCOETIDAE	**Flying Fish**
Cheilopogon furcatus (Mitchill, 1815)	flying fish
Hirundichthys sp.	unidentified *Hirundichthys* species
HEMIRAMPHIDAE	**Halfbeaks**
Hyporamphus acutus acutus (Günther, 1871)	Pacific halfbeak
APOGONIDAE	**Cardinalfishes**
Apogon angustatus (Smith & Radcliffe in Radcliffe, 1911)	broad-striped cardinalfish
Apogon apogonides (Bleeker, 1856)	cardinalfish
Cheilodipterus quinquelineatus (Cuvier *in* Cuvier & Valenciennes, 1828)	five-lined cardinalfish
Apogon susanae (Greenfield, 2001)	cardinalfish
Apogon taeniophorus (Regan, 1908)	cardinalfish
CARANGIDAE	**Jacks and Trevallys**
Alectis ciliaris (Bloch, 1787)	threadfin pompano
Carangoides ferdau (Forsskål, 1775)	bar jack
Carangoides orthogrammus (Jordan & Gilbert 1882)	yellow-spotted trevally
Caranx ignobilis (Forsskål, 1775)	giant trevally
Caranx lugubris (Poey, 1860)	black jack
Carnax melampygus	bluefin trevally

Scientific Name	Common Name
(Cuvier *in* Cuvier & Valenciennes, 1833)	
Caranx sexfasciatus (Quoy & Gaimard, 1825)	bigeye trevally
Elegatis bipinnulata (Quoy & Gaimard, 1825)	rainbow runner
Naucrates ductor (Linnaeus, 1758)	jack
Scomberoides lysan (Forsskål, 1775)	leatherback
LUTJANIDAE	**Snappers**
Aphareus furca (Lacepède, 1801)	blue small-tooth jobfish
Lutjanus bohar (Forsskål, 1775)	twinspot snapper, redspot snapper
Lutjanus fulvus (Forster *in* Bloch & Schneider, 1801)	flametail snapper
Lutjanus gibbus (Forsskål, 1775)	humpback snapper
Lutjanus kasmira (Forsskål, 1775)	blue-lined snapper
Lutjanus monostigma (Cuvier *in* Cuvier & Valenciennes, 1828)	one-spot snapper
CAESIONIDAE	**Fusiliers**
Caesio teres (Seale, 1906)	yellow-back fusilier
LETHRINIDAE	**Emperors**
Gnathodentex aureolineatus (Lacepède, 1802)	yellowspot emperor
Lethrinus olivaceus (Valenciennes *in* Cuvier & Valenciennes, 1830)	olive emperor
Monotaxis grandoculis (Forsskål, 1775)	bigeye emperor
MULLIDAE	**Goatfishes**
Mulloides mimicus (Randall & Guézé, 1980)	mimic goatfish
Parupeneus bifasciatus (Lacepède, 1801)	two-barred goatfish
Parupeneus cyclostomus (Lacepède, 1801)	yellowsaddle goatfish
Parupeneus trifasciatus (Lacepède, 1801)	three-barred goatfish
PEMPHERIDAE	**Sweepers**
Pempheris oualensis (Cuvier *in* Cuvier & Valenciennes, 1831)	bronze sweeper
KYPHOSIDAE	**Rudderfishes & Sea Chubs**
Kyphosus cinerascens (Forsskål, 1775)	highfin rudderfish, snubnose rudderfish
Kyphosus vaigiensis (Quoy & Gaimard, 1825)	lowfin rudderfish, brassy chub
Kyphosus sp.	unidentified *Kyphosus* species
CHAETODONTIDAE	**Butterflyfishes**
Chaetodon auriga (Forsskål, 1775)	threadfin butterflyfish
Chaetodon lineolatus (Cuvier (ex Quoy & Gaimard) *in* Cuvier & Valenciennes, 1831)	lined butterflyfish
Chaetodon lunula (Lacépède, 1802)	racoon butterflyfish
Chaetodon meyeri (Bloch & Schneider, 1801)	Meyer's butterflyfish
Chaedodon ornatissimus (Cuvier (ex Solander) *in* Cuvier & Valenciennes, 1831)	ornate butterflyfish
Chaetodon quadrimaculatus (Gray, 1831)	fourspot butterflyfish

Scientific Name	Common Name
Chaetodon unimaculatus (Bloch, 1787)	teardrop butterflyfish
Forcipiger flavissimus (Jordan & McGregor in Jordan & Evermann, 1898)	long-nosed butterflyfish
Hemitaurichthys thompsoni (Fowler, 1923)	Thompson's butterflyfish
POMACANTHIDAE	**Angelfishes**
Apolemichthys griffisi (Carlson & Taylor, 1981)	Griffith's angelfish
Apolemichthys xanthopunctatus (Burgess, 1973)	golden-spotted angelfish
Centropyge flavissima (Cuvier in Cuvier & Valenciennes, 1831)	lemon-peel angelfish
Centropyge loricula (Günther, 1874)	flame angelfish
Pomacanthus imperator (Bloch, 1787)	emporer angelfish
POMACENTRIDAE	**Damselfishes**
Abudefduf septemfasciatus (Cuvier in Cuvier & Valenciennes, 1830)	banded sergeant
Abudefduf sordidus (Forsskål, 1775)	black-spot sergeant
Chromis acares (Randall & Swerdloff, 1973)	midget chromis
Chromis agilis (Smith, 1960)	bronze reef chromis
Chromis margaritifer (Fowler, 1946)	bicolor chromis
Chromis vanderbilti (Fowler, 1941)	Vanderbilt's chromis
Chromis xanthura (Bleeker, 1854)	black chromis
Chrysiptera cyanea (Quoy & Gaimard, 1825)	blue devil
Chrysiptera glauca (Cuvier in Cuvier & Valenciennes, 1830)	gray demoiselle
Lepidozygus tapeinosoma (Bleeker, 1856)	fusilier damsel
Plectroglyphidodon dickii (Liénard, 1839)	Dick's damsel
Plectroglyphidodon imparipennis (Vaillant & Sauvage, 1875)	bright-eye damsel
Plectroglyphidodon johnstonianus (Fowler & Ball, 1924)	Johnston Island damsel
Plectroglyphid. phoenixensis (Schultz, 1943)	Phoenix Islands damsel
Pomacentrus bankanensis (Bleeker, 1853)	speckled damsel
Pomacentrus coelestis (Jordan & Starks, 1901)	neon damsel
Stegastes sp. or *Pomacentrus* sp.	unidentified damselfish (brown head and anterior body, pale caudal area)
Stegastes sp.	unidentified *Stegastes* species, gregory
Stegastes aureus (Fowler, 1927)	golden gregory
Stegastes fasciolatus (Ogilby, 1889)	Pacific gregory
Stegastes nigricans (Lacepède, 1802)	dusky farmfish
KUHLIIDAE	**Flagtails**

Scientific Name	Common Name
Kuhlia petiti (Schultz, 1943)	flagtail
Kuhlia sandvicensis (Steindachner, 1876)	Hawaiian flagtail
Kuhlia sp.	unidentified *Kuhlia* species
CIRRHITIDAE	**Hawkfishes**
Cirrhitichthys oxycephalus (Bleeker, 1855)	pixy hawkfish
Neocirrhites armatus (Castelnau, 1873)	flame hawkfish
Paracirrhites arcatus (Cuvier *in* Cuvier & Valenciennes, 1829)	arc-eye hawkfish
Paracirrhites forsteri (Schneider *in* Bloch & Schneider, 1801)	freckled hawkfish, blackside hawkfish
Paracirrhites hemistictus (Günther, 1874)	whitespot hawkfish
Paracirrhites xanthus (Randall, 1963)	yellow hawkfish
SPHYRAENIDAE	**Barracudas**
Sphyraena sp.	unidentified *Sphyraena* species
Sphyraena barracuda (Walbaum, 1792)	great barracuda
Sphyraena qenie (Klunziger, 1870)	blackfin barracuda
LABRIDAE	**Wrasses**
Anampses caeruleopunctatus (Rüppell, 1829)	blue-spotted wrasse
Anampses melanurus (Bleeker, 1857)	wrasse
Anampses meleagrides (Valenciennes *in* Cuvier & Valenciennes, 1840)	yellowtail wrasse
Bodianus axillaries (Bennett, 1832)	axilspot hogfish
Bodianus loxozonus (Snyder, 1908)	blackfin hogfish
Bodianus prognathus (Lobel, 1981)	hogfish
Cheilinus trilobatus (Lacepède, 1801)	tripletail wrasse
Cheilinus undulatus (Rüppell, 1835)	humphead wrasse, Napoleonfish, Napoleon wrasse
Cirrhilabrus exquisitus (Smith, 1957)	exquisite wrasse
Coris aygula (Lacepède, 1801)	clown coris
Coris centralis (Randall, 1999)	coris
Coris gaimard (Quoy & Gaimard, 1824)	yellowtail coris
Epibulus insidiator (Pallas, 1770)	slingjaw wrasse
Gomphosus varius (Lacepède, 1801)	bird wrasse
Halichoeres hortulanus (Lacepède, 1801)	checkerboard wrasse
Halichoeres melasmopomus (Randall, 1981)	black-ear wrasse
Halichoeres ornatissinus (Garrett, 1863)	ornate wrasse fish
Halichoeres pallidus (Kuiter & Randall, 1995)	wrasse
Halichoeres trimaculatus (Quoy & Gaimard, 1834)	three-spot wrasse
Hemigymnus fasciatus (Bloch, 1792)	barred thicklip wrasse
Hologymnosus annulatus (Lacepède, 1801)	ring wrasse

Scientific Name	Common Name
Labroides bicolor (Fowler & Bean, 1928)	bicolor cleaner wrasse
Labroides dimidiatus (Valenciennes *in* Cuvier & Valenciennes, 1839)	bluestreak cleaner wrasse
Labroides rubrolabiatus (Randall, 1958)	cleaner wrasse
Labropsis xanthonota (Randall, 1981)	wedge-tailed wrasse
Macropharyngodon meleagris (Valenciennes *in* Cuvier & Valenciennes, 1839)	leopard wrasse
Oxycheilinus unifasciatus (Streets, 1877)	wrasse
Pseudocheilinus hexataenia (Bleeker, 1857)	sixline wrasse
Pseudocheilinus octotaenia (Jenkins, 1901)	eightline wrasse
Pseudocheilinus tetrataenia (Schultz in Schultz et al., 1960)	fourline wrasse
Pseudocoris heteroptera (Bleeker, 1857)	wrasse
Pseudodax mollucanus (Valenciennes *in* Cuvier & Valenciennes, 1840)	Wrasse
Pseudojuloides cerasinus (Snyder, 1904)	smalltail wrasse
Stethojulis bandanensis (Bleeker, 1851)	redshoulder wrasse
Thalassoma amblycephalum (Bleeker, 1856)	twotone wrasse
Thalassoma lutescens (Lay & Bennett (ex Solander), 1839)	sunset wrasse
Thalassoma purpureum (Forsskål, 1775)	surge wrasse
Thalassoma quinquevittatum (Lay & Bennett, 1839)	fivestripe surge wrasse
Thalassoma trilobatum (Lacepède, 1801)	Christmas wrasse
SCARIDAE	**Parrotfishes**
Bolbometopon muricatum (Valenciennes *in* Cuvier & Valenciennes, 1840)	humphead parrotfish, bumphead parrotfish
Calatomus carolinus (Valenciennes, 1840)	bucktooth parrotfish, stareye parrotfish
Chlorurus frontalis (Valenciennes *in* Cuvier & Valenciennes, 1840)	tan-faced parrotfish
Chlorurus microrhinus (Bleeker, 1854)	parrotfish
Chlorurus sordidus (Forsskål, 1775)	bullethead parrotfish
Scarus altipinnis (Steindachner, 1879)	filament-finned parrotfish
Scarus frenatus (Lacepède, 1802)	vermiculate parrotfish
Scarus ghobban (Forsskål, 1775)	blue-barred parrotfish
Scarus globiceps (Valenciennes *in* Cuvier & Valenciennes, 1840)	roundhead parrotfish
Scarus oviceps (Valenciennes in Cuvier & Valenciennes, 1840)	dark-capped parrotfish
Scarus rubroviolaceus (Bleeker, 1847)	red and violet parrotfish, redlip parrotfish
Scarus tricolor (Bleeker, 1847)	tricolor parrotfish
CREEDIIDAE	**Sand Burrowers**

Scientific Name	Common Name
Crystallodytes cookei enderburyensis (Schultz, 1943)	sand burrower
TRIPTERYGIIDAE	**Triplefins**
Enneapterygius nigricada (Fricke, 1997)	triplefin
BLENNIIDAE	**Blennies**
Blenniidae sp.	unidentified blenny species
Aspidontus taeniatus (Quoy & Gaimard, 1834)	cleaner mimic
Blenniella gibbifrons (Quoy & Gaimard, 1824)	blenny
Blenniella paula (Bryan & Herre, 1903)	blenny
Cirripectes quagga (Fowler & Ball, 1924)	squiggly blenny
Cirripectes variolosus (Valenciennes *in* Cuvier & Valenciennes, 1836)	red-speckled blenny
Cirripectes sp.	Unidentified *Cirripectes* species
Ecsenius midas (Starck, 1969)	blenny
Entomacrodus cymatobiotus (Schultz & Chapman, 1960)	blenny
Entomacrodus sealei (Bryan & Herre, 1903)	Seale's rockskipper
Entomacrodus striatus (Quoy & Gaimard, 1836)	pearly rockskipper
Entomacrodus thalassinus thalassinus (Jordan & Seale, 1906)	reef margin blenny
Istiblennius edentulous (Schneider *in* Bloch & Schneider, 1801)	rippled rockskipper
Plagiotremus rhynorhynchus (Bleeker, 1852)	blue-striped blenny
Plagiotremus tapeinosoma (Bleeker, 1857)	piano blenny, scale-eating blenny
Rhabdoblennius sp.	unidentified *Rhabdoblennius* species
CALLIONYMIDAE	**Dragonets**
Callionymidae sp.	unidentified dragonet species (probably *Synchiropus* sp.)
GOBIIDAE	**Gobies**
Gobiidae sp.	unidentified goby species (reported 2001)
Amblygobius phalaena (Valenciennes in Cuvier & Valenciennes, 1837)	brown-barred goby
Eviota zonura (Jordan & Seale, 1906)	zoned pygmy goby
Priolepis squamogena (Winterbottom & Burridge, 1989)	goby
Valenciennea strigata (Broussonet, 1782)	blue-streak goby
ACANTHURIDAE	**Surgeonfishes & Unicornfishes**
Acanthurus achilles (Shaw, 1803)	Achilles tang
Acanthurus blochii (Valenciennes in Cuvier &	ringtail surgeonfish

Scientific Name	Common Name
Valenciennes, 1835)	
Acanthurus guttatus (Forster *in* Bloch & Schneider, 1801)	spotted surgeonfish
Acanthurus leucochilus (Herre, 1927)	pale-lipped surgeonfish
Acanthurus lineatus (Linnaeus, 1758)	blue-banded surgeonfish
Acanthurus mata (Cuvier, 1829)	elongate surgeonfish
Acanthurus nigricans (Linnaeus, 1758)	whitecheek surgeonfish
Acanthurus nigricauda (Duncker & Mohr,1929)	epaulette surgeonfish
Acanthurus nigrofuscus (Forsskål, 1775)	brown surgeonfish
Acanthurus nigroris (Valenciennes *in* Cuvier & Valenciennes 1835)	blue-lined surgeonfish
Acanthurus olivaceus (Bloch & Schneider (ex Forster), 1801)	orangeband surgeonfish
Acanthurus rackliffei (*A. achilles* x *A. nigricans*)(Schultz, 1943)	hybrid surgeonfish
Acanthurus triostegus (Linnaeus, 1758)	convict tang
Acanthurus thompsoni (Fowler, 1923)	Thompson's surgeonfish
Acanthurus xanthopterus (Valenciennes *in* Cuvier & Valenciennes, 1835)	yellow-finned surgeonfish
Ctenochaetus sp.	unidentified *Ctenochaetus* species
Ctenochaetus cyanocheilus (Randall & Clements, 2001)	Surgeonfish
Ctenochaetus flavicaudis (Fowler, 1938)	surgeonfish
Ctenochaetus hawaiiensis (Randall, 1955)	chevron tang, black surgeonfish
Ctenochaetus marginatus (Valenciennes in Cuvier & Valenciennes, 1835)	blue-spotted bristletooth
Ctenochaetus striatus (Quoy & Gaimard, 1825)	striped bristletooth
Naso brevirostris (Valenciennes in Cuvier & Valenciennes, 1835)	spotted unicornfish
Naso hexacanthus (Bleeker, 1855)	black-tongue unicornfish, sleek unicornfish
Naso lituratus (Forster in Bloch & Schneider, 1801)	liturate surgeonfish
Naso vlamingii (Valenciennes in Cuvier & Valenciennes, 1835)	bignose unicornfish
Zebrasoma rostratum (Günther, 1873)	tang
Zebrasoma scopas (Cuvier, 1829)	brown tang
EPHIPPIDAE	**Batfishes**
Platax sp.	unidentified *Platax* species
Platax teira (Forsskål, 1775)	longfin spadefish

Scientific Name	Common Name
ZANCLIDAE	**Moorish Idol**
Zanclus cornutus (Linnaeus, 1758)	moorish idol
SCOMBRIDAE	**Tunas**
Euthynnus affinis (Cantor, 1849)	kawakawa, bonito
Gymnosarda unicolor (Rüppell, 1836)	dogtooth tuna
NOMEIDAE	**Driftfishes, Man-of-war Fishes, and Shepherdfishes**
Nomeidae sp.	unidentified Nomeidae species
Psenes cyanophrys (Valenciennes *in* Cuvier & Valenciennes, 1833)	freckled driftfish
BOTHIDAE	**Left-hand Flounders**
Bothus mancus (Broussonet, 1782)	peacock flounder
BALISTIDAE	**Triggerfishes**
Balistapus undulatus (Park, 1797)	orangestriped triggerfish
Balistoides viridescens (Bloch & Schneider, 1801)	mustache triggerfish, titan triggerfish
Melichtys niger (Bloch, 1786)	black triggerfish
Melichtys vidua (Richardson (ex Solander), 1845)	pinktail triggerfish
Odonus niger (Rüppell, 1836)	redtooth triggerfish
Pseudobalistes flavimarginatus (Rüppell,1829)	yellowmargin triggerfish
Rhinecanthus rectangulus (Bloch & Schneider, 1801)	wedge picassofish, humunukunukuapua'a
Sufflamen bursa (Bloch & Schneider, 1801)	scythe triggerfish, boomerang triggerfish
Sufflamen chrysopterus (Bloch & Schneider, 1801)	halfmoon triggerfish
Xanthichthys caeruleolineatus (Randall, Matsuura, & Zama, 1978)	bluelined triggerfish
MONACANTHIDAE	**Filefishes & Leatherjackets**
Aluterus scriptus (Osbeck. 1765)	scribbled filefish
Amanses scopas (Cuvier, 1829)	broom filefish
Cantherhines dumerilii (Hollard, 1854)	barred filefish
Cantherhines pardalis (Rüppell, 1837)	wire-net filefish
Pervagor marginalis (Hutchins, 1986)	blackbar filefish
OSTRACIIDAE	**Trunkfishes**
Ostracion meleagris meleagris (Shaw *in* Shaw & Nodder, 1796)	spotted trunkfish
TETRAODONTIDAE	**Puffers**
Arothron meleagris (Lacepède (ex Commerson), 1798)	guineafowl puffer
Canthigaster amboinensis (Bleeker, 1865)	Ambon sharpnose puffer

Scientific Name	Common Name
Canthigaster janthinoptera (Bleeker, 1855)	puffer
Canthigaster solandri (Richardson (ex Solander), 1845)	spotted sharpnose puffer
DIODONTIDAE	**Porcupinefishes**
Diodon hystrix (Linnaeus, 1758)	porcupinefish

Table B-3: Plant species of Jarvis Island NWR. Compiled from unpublished USFWS trip reports.

Scientific Name	Common Name, (Hawaiian Name)	Source*	Observed in 2004
Cocos nucifera	coconut, (nui)	I	no
Pandanus sp.	pandanus, (hala)	I	no
Eragristus whitneyi	native lovegrass	N	yes
Lepturus repens	Pacific Island thintail, wiry bunchgrass	N	yes
Fimbristylis cymosa	buttonsedge	N	no
Boerhavia tetranda	(alena)	N	yes
Portulaca lutea	portulaca, ('ihi)	N	yes
Sesuvium portulacastrum	sea purslane	N	yes
Tribulus cistoides	puncturevine, (nohu)	N	yes
Abutilon indicum	Indian mallow	A	yes
Sida fallax	('ilima)	A	yes

*Source: N = native, I = introduced, A = accidentally introduced

Note: Various cultivated crop plants including cabbage, onion, radish, celery, peanut, lettuce, zinnia, phlox, marigold, white bean, avocado, plum and date plum were planted during occupation periods. None of these plants were observed in 2004.

Table B-4: Birds of Jarvis Island NWR. Numbers are counts of adult birds only and compiled from unpublished USFWS trip reports. Note: No bird species found on Jarvis are listed according to the Endangered Species Act.

Scientific Name	Common Name	Highest count since 1973	Birds of Conservation Concern Status[b]	National Shorebird Prioritization Category[a]	Regional Seabird Conservation Category[c]
Nesofregetta fuliginosa	Polynesian storm-petrel	3	BCC 68		Highly Imperiled
Puffinus nativitatis	Christmas Shearwater*	20	BCC 68		High Concern
Puffinus lhermineri	Audubon's Shearwater*	20			High Concern
Puffinus pacificus	wedge-tailed shearwater*	41			Low
Phaethon rubricauda	red-tailed tropicbird*	2,500			Moderate
Sula dactylatra	masked booby*	7,000			Moderate
Sula leucogaster	brown booby*	2,000			Moderate
Sula sula	red-footed booby*	1,000			Currently not at Risk
Fregata minor	great frigatebird*	2,400			Moderate
Fregata ariel	lesser frigatebird*	4,000	BCC 68		High Concern
Onychoprion lunatus	gray-backed tern*	1,100			Moderate
Onychoprion fuscatus	sooty tern*	1,000,000+			Moderate
Anous stolidus	brown noddy*	10,000			Currently not at Risk
Procelsterna cerulea	blue noddy*	650	BCC 68		High Concern
Gygis alba	white tern*	11			Moderate
Pluvialis fulva	Pacific golden-plover	117	BCC 68	High Concern	

Scientific Name	Common Name	Highest count since 1973	Birds of Conservation Concern Status[b]	National Shorebird Prioritization Category[a]	Regional Seabird Conservation Category[c]
Numenius tahitiensis	bristle-thighed curlew	51	BCC 68	High Concern	
Arenaria interpres	ruddy turnstone	20		High Concern	
Calidris alba	sanderling	2		High Concern	
Anas acuta	northern pintail	1			

*indicates documented breeding species on Jarvis

[a]Species prioritization categories according to United States Shorebird Conservation Plan (Brown et al. 2000)

[b]Birds of Conservation Concern status according to Birds of Conservation Concern 2002 (U.S. Fish and Wildlife Service 2002).

[c]Conservation classification according to Seabird Conservation Plan, Pacific Region (Englis and Naughton 2004)

This page left intentionally blank.

Appendix C

List of Cited References

Ashmole, N.P. and M.J Ashmole. 1967. Comparative Feeding Ecology of Sea Birds of a Tropical Oceanic Island. Peabody Museum of Natural History, Yale University Bulletin 24.

Atomic Energy Commission. 1963. Reconnaissance Survey Report: Howland, Baker & Canton Islands. Las Vegas, NV.

Boehlert, G., editor. 1993. Fisheries of Hawaii and the U.S. associated Pacific Islands. Marine Fisheries Review 55:1-138.

Brown, D, N. M. K. Y. Kahanu, S.K. Kikiloi, T.K. Tengan and J. Zisk. 2002. Hui Panalā'au. Bishop Museum, Honolulu, published pamphlet, 16 pp.

Brown, S. C. Hickey, and B. Harrington eds. 2000. The U.S. Shorebird Conservation Plan. Manomet Center for Conservation Sciences, Manomet, MA.

Browne, A.C. 1940. Proc. Hawaiian Ent. Soc. 10(3):369.

Bryan, E.H., Jr. 1974. Panala'au Memoirs. Pacific Scientific Information Center. Bernice P. Bishop Museum, Honolulu, HI.

Christophersen, E. 1927. Vegetation of Pacific Equatorial Islands. Bernice P. Bishop Museum Bulletin 44: No. 2. 79 p.

Citta, John and Michelle H. Reynolds. 2006. Draft Seabird Monitoring Assessment for Hawaii and the Pacific Islands . Migratory Birds and Habitat Programs USFWS. USGS-BRD 183 pp.

D'Arrigo, R, R. Wilson, C. Deser, G. Wiles, E. Cook, R. Villalba, A. Tudhope, J. Cole, and B. Linsley. 2005. Tropical – North Pacific climate linkages over the past four centuries. Journal of Climate 18: 5253-5265.

Darwin, C. 1842. The structure and distribution of coral reefs. Smith Elder, London. 214 pp., 2 pls.

Depkin, C. and C; Newton. 1995. Howland Island Trip Report 22-25 March 1995. Administrative Report. U.S. Fish and Wildlife Service, Honolulu, HI.96850.

Diamond, A.W. 1978. Feeding strategies and population size in tropical seabirds. American Naturalist 112:215-223.

Emory, K. P., 1939. Archaeology of the Phoenix Islands. Hawaii Academy of Science Proceedings. Special Publication 34. Bishop Museum, Honolulu, Hawaii.

Engilis, Jr., A. and M. Naughton. 2004. U.S. Pacific Islands Regional Shorebird Conservation Plan. U.S. Shorebird Conservation Plan. U.S. Department of the Interior, Fish and Wildlife Service. Portland, Oregon.

Fefer, S.I., C.S. Harrison, M.B. Naughton, and R.J. Shallenberger. 1984. Synopsis of results of recent seabird research conducted in the Northwestern Hawaiian Islands. Proc. Res. Inv. NWHI UNIHI-SEAGRANT-MR-84-01

Flint, E. and D. Woodside. 1993. Howland and Baker Islands Trip Report, 19 January to 15 February, 1993. Administrative Report, U.S. Fish and Wildlife Service, Honolulu, HI 96850.

Flint, E. and C. Eggleston. 2004. Draft Equatorial Refuges Trip Report. January 8-31, 2004. Administrative Report. U.S. Fish and Wildlife Service, Honolulu, HI

Floros, C. D., M. J. Samways, and B. Armstrong. 2004. Taxonomic patterns of bleaching within a South African coral assemblage. Biodiversity and Conservation. 13: 1175-1194.Fowler. 1927. Hague, J.D. 1862. On phosphatic guano islands of the Pacific Ocean. Amer. Jour. Sci., 84: 224-243, 1862.

Gove, J.M., M.A. Merrifield and R.E. Brainard. 2006. Temporal Variability of current-driven upwelling of Jarvis Island. J. Geophys. Res. 111(C12): C12011.

Harrison, C.S., T. S. Hida, M.P. Seki. 1983. Hawaiian Seabird Feeding Ecology. Wildlife Monographs 85:1-71.

Hutchinson, G.E. 1950. The Biochemistry of Vertebrate Excretion. Bull. Amer. Museum Nat. Hist. 96. 554 p.

IPCC, Ed., 2001. Climate Change 2001: The Scientific Basis, Contribution of Working Group I to the Third Assessment Report of the Intergovernmental Panel on Climate Change. Cambridge Univ. Press, Cambridge, UK, 881 pp.

Johannes, R.E. 1981. Words of the Lagoon: Fishing and marine lore in the Palau District of Micronesia. University of California Press, Berkeley.

Ketaing, B.H. 1992. Insular geology of the Line Islands, in Keating, B.H., B. Bolton. Eds. Geology and offshore mineral resources of the Central Pacific Basin. Circum Pacific Council En. And Min. Res., Earth Sciences, Monograph Series.

Kirby, H. 1925. The birds of Fanning Island, Central Pacific Ocean. The Condor 23: 185-196.

King, W.B. 1970. The trade wind zone oceanography pilot study. Part VII: observations of seabirds March 1964 to June 1965. U.S. Fish and Wildl. Ser. Spec. Sci. Rep. - Fish. 586. 136pp.

Kirkpatrick R.D. and M.J. Rauzon. 1986. Foods of Feral Cats *Felis catus* on Jarvis and Howland Islands, Central Pacific Ocean. Biotropica 18 (1): 72-75.

Maude, H. E. 1961. Post-Spanish discoveries in the central Pacific. Jour. Pol. Soc. 70(1):67-111.

Maragos, J.E., and P.L. Jokiel 1978. Reef Corals of Canton Atoll: I. Zoogeography. In: Naval Undersea Center Technical Publication 395:55-70, and *Atoll Research Bulletin* 221:55-70 (Sept 1978)

Michener, W. K., E. R. Blood, K. L. Bildstein, M. M. Brinson, and L. R. Gardner. 1997. Climate change, hurricanes and tropical storms and rising sea level in coastal wetlands. Ecological Applications. 7:770-801.

Mueller-Dombois, D. and F. R. Fosberg. 1998. Vegetation of the Tropical Island Pacific. Springer-Verlag, New York (Book in collection of H. Freifeld, 3-122 Federal Building).

Morrison, R.J. 1990. Pacific Atoll Soils: Chemistry, Mineralogy and Classification. Atoll Research Bulletin. No. 339: 25p.

Mundy, B., R. Wass, E. DeMartini, B. Greene, B. Zgliczynski, and R. Schroeder. 2002. Inshore fishes of Howland Island, Baker Island, Jarvis Island, Palmyra Atoll, and Kingman Reef. Unpublished ms. Pacific Islands Fisheries Science Center, Honolulu, 80 pp.

Munro, G.C. 1924. (unpublished) Report of the ornithologist on the USS Whippoorwill expedition trip "B" to Howland and Baker Islands. Sept. 15 to Oct. 7, 1924. (Extracted Aug. 4, 1965, by Roger Clapp)

National Marine Fisheries Service and U.S. Fish and Wildlife Service. 1998. Recovery Plan for U.S. Pacific Populations of the Green Turtle (*Chelonia mydas*). National Marine Fisheries Service, Silver Springs, MD.

National Marine Fisheries Service and U.S. Fish and Wildlife Service. 1998. Recovery Plan for U.S. Pacific Populations of the Hawksbill Turtle (*Eretmochelys imbricate*). National Marine Fisheries Service, Silver Springs, MD.

NOAA 1991. Climates of the World. Historical Climatology Series 6-4. National Oceanic and Atmospheric Administration, National Climatic Data Center, Asheville, N.C. p. 26.

Overpeck, J.T., B.L. Otto-Bliesner, G.H. Miller, D.R. Muhs, R.B. Alley, and J.T. Kiehl. 2006. Paleoclimatic Evidence for Future Ice-Sheet Instability and Rapid Sea-Level Rise. Science 311:1747-1750.

Rauzon, M. J. 1990. Expedition Report: Jarvis Island National Wildlife Refuge. Administrative Report. U.S. Fish and Wildlife Service, Honolulu, Hawaii.

Rauzon, M.J. and A.S. Wegmann. 2004. Expedition to the Line Islands. Jarvis Island, Palmyra Atoll, Kingman Reef terrestrial surveys. Administrative Report. U.S. Fish and Wildife Service, Honolulu, HI.
Rauzon, M.J. and D.H. Woodside. 1998. Howland Island Trip Report26 4-9 March 1998. Administrative Report. U.S. Fish and Wildlife Service, Honolulu, Hawaii.

Shun, Kanalei. 1987. Archaeological Reconnaissance Site Survey and Limited Subsurface of Baker and Howland Islands Final Report: Prepared for US Army Engineer District, Honolulu Corps of Engineers, Fort Shafter, Hawaii.

Shea, E. L, G. Dolcemascolo, C. L. Anderson, A. Barnston, C. P. Guard, M. P. Hamnett, S. T. Kubota, N. Lewis, J. Loschnigg, and G. Meehl. 2001. Preparing for a Changing Climate: The potential Consequences of Climate Variability and Change. Published Report. East-West Center, Honolulu, Hawaii. 100 pp.

Sibley, F.C. R.B. Clapp, and C.R. Long. 1965. Biological Survey of Howland Island, March 1963 – May 1965. Unpublished Report of Pacific Ocean Biological Survey Program, Division of Birds Smithsonian Institution, Washington D.C.

Skaggs, J. M., 1994. The Great Guano Rush. Entrepreneurs and American Overseas Expansion. St. Martin's Griffin. New York.

Smith, S.V and R. M. Buddemeier. 1992. Global Change and Coral Reef Ecosystems. Annual Review of Ecology and Systematics. 23:89-118.

Starbuck, A., 1878. History of the American whale fishery from its earliest inception to the year 1876. In Report of the Commissioner of Fish and Fisheries for 1875-1876. Washington, Government Printing Office. Pp. 1-779.

Townsend, C.H. 1935. The distribution of certain whales as shown by logbook records of American whaleships. Zoolologica 19:3-50.

UNESCO World Heritage Centre. 2003. Central Pacific World Heritage Project International Workshop Report, 2-6 June 2003, Honolulu, Hawaii, USA. Paris, 44pp.

UNESCO World Heritage Centre. 2004. Central Pacific World Heritage Project, National Workshop Report, 5-11 October 2004, Kiritimati Island, the Republic of Kiribati. Paris, 11pp.

U.S. Atomic Energy Commission (USAEC). 1963. Reconnaissance Survey Report. Howland, Baker & Canton Islands. October, 1963. U.S. Atomic Energy Commission, Nevada Operations Office. Prepared by: Holmes & Narver Inc. Logistics Planning Group. Las Vegas, Nevada.

U. S. Fish and Wildlife Service. 1973. Baker Island, Howland Island, and Jarvis Island National Wildlife Refuges, Biological Ascertainment Reports.

U. S. Fish and Wildlife Service. 1975. Baker Island, Howland Island, and Jarvis Island National Wildlife Refuges, Narrative Report, FY 1975. Kailua, HI

U.S. Fish and Wildlife Service. 1981. Refuge Manual. Wash., D.C.

U.S. Fish and Wildlife Service. 1998a. Coral Reef Initiative in the Pacific: Howland Island, Baker Island, and Jarvis Island National Wildlife Refuges. Honolulu, HI.

U. S. Fish and Wildlife Service. 1998b. Remote islands ecosystem plan: Howland Island, Baker Island, and Jarvis Island National Wildlife Refuges. Honolulu, HI. 16 pp.

U.S. Fish and Wildlife Service. 2000. Pacific Remote Islands National Wildlife Refuge Complex Special Conditions & Rules for Moving Between Islands and Atolls and Packing for Field Camps. Honolulu, HI.

U.S. Fish and Wildlife Service. 2001. Environmental Assessment: Proposed Palmyra Atoll National Wildlife Refuge, Line Islands, Central Pacific Ocean. Portland, OR.

U.S. Fish and Wildlife Service. 2002. Birds of Conservation Concern. Arlington, Va.

U.S. Fish and Wildlife Service. 2005. Regional Seabird Conservation Plan, Pacific Region. U.S. Fish and Wildlife Service, Migratory Birds and Habitat Programs, Pacific Region, Portland, Oregon.

Vitousek, M. J., Kilonsky, B, and W. G. Leslie. 1980. Meteorological Observations in the Line Islands, 1972-1980. Honolulu, HI. 74 pp.

Vitousek, P. M. 1994. Beyond global warming: ecology and global change. Ecology. 75:1861-1876.

This page left intentionally blank.

Appendix D

Quarantine Protocol for Jarvis Island NWR

The following protocol was developed to maintain consistency in quarantine procedures for all NWRs in the Pacific. Thus, these provisions apply to all of the remote island national wildlife refuges. Some refuges, including Jarvis, may have additional restrictions and requirements.

Pacific Remote Islands National Wildlife Refuge Complex
Special Conditions and Rules for
Moving Between Islands and Atolls and
Packing for Field Camps

The islands and atolls of the Pacific Remote Islands National Wildlife Refuge Complex are special places providing habitat for many rare, endemic plants and animals. Many of these species are formally listed as federally Threatened or Endangered under the Endangered Species Act of 1973. Endemic plants and insects, and the predators they support, are especially vulnerable to the introduction of competing or consuming, non-native species. Such introductions may cause the extinction of island endemics, or even the destruction of entire island ecological communities. Notable local examples include: the introduction of rabbits to Laysan Island in 1902 which caused the extinction of numerous plant and insect species and 3 endemic landbird species; the introduction of rats to many Pacific Islands causing the elimination of many burrowing seabird colonies; the introduction of the annual grass, sandbur, to Laysan Island where it has out competed native bunch grass and eliminated nesting habitat for the Endangered Laysan finch; and the introduction and proliferation of numerous ant species throughout the Pacific Islands to the widespread detriment of endemic plant and insect species (refuge files).

Several of the islands within the Refuge Complex are especially pristine, and, as a result, are diverse in terms of rare and special declining native plants and animals. Nihoa Island has 13 potential candidate Endangered insect species, numerous Endangered plants, and 2 Endangered birds. Necker Island has Endangered plants and 7 endemic insects that are candidates for the Endangered Species List. Laysan Island has endangered plants, five potential candidates endangered insect species and the Endangered Laysan finch and Laysan duck. Other islands in the Refuge Complex such as Lisianski, Howland, Baker, and Jarvis and islets in Atolls such as Rose, Pearl and Hermes Reef and French Frigate Shoals are inhabited by a variety of endemic and/or endangered species and require special protection from invasive species.

Other Pacific Island such as Kure and the "high islands" (Oahu, Hawaii, Maui, Kauai, etc.) as well as, certain islands within Midway Atoll, Pearl and Hermes Reef and French Frigate Shoals have native plants and animals that are at high risk from introduction to the relatively pristine islands discussed above. Of special concerns are introductions of non-native snakes, rats, ants and a variety of other insect and plant species. Invasive plants of highest concern are *Verbesina encelioides, Cenchrus echinatus, and Setaria verticillata.*

The U. S. Fish and Wildlife Service is responsible for the management and protection of the fish, wildlife, plants, and their habitats associated with islands of the Pacific Remote Islands NWR Complex. No one is permitted to access any of the Refuge's islands without the express written permission of the Refuge Manager in the form of a Special Use Permit. Because of the above concerns, the following restrictions on the movement of personnel and materials to the islands of the Refuge Complex exist.

With the exception of Tern Island, French Frigate Shoals, the following rules apply:

Clothing and Soft Gear:

- Any personnel landing boats at any island should have clean clothes and shoes, meaning that they are free of dirt and seeds.

- Any personnel going ashore at any island and moving inshore from the immediate area in which waves are breaking at the time of landing must have new footwear, new or island-specific clothes and new or island-specific soft gear that have been frozen (<4 C) for at least 48 hours.

- At the discretion of the local USFWS representative, personnel from a NOAA ship or any other vessel servicing the Refuge may be allowed on shore to visit pre-designated areas for guided tours. All stipulations for clean and frozen clothes apply.

- Otherwise, any personnel entering any vegetated area, regardless of how sparse the vegetation, must have new footwear, new clothes and new soft gear all frozen for at least 48 hours.

Definitions:

- "new" means off the shelf and never used anywhere but the island in question.
- "clothing" is all apparel, shoes, socks, over and under garments.
- "soft gear" is all gear such as daypacks, fanny packs, camera bags, camera/binocular straps, microphone covers, nets, holding or weighing bags, bedding, tents, luggage, or any fabric or material capable of harboring seeds or insects.

During transit, clothing and gear coming off Kure, Midway, and Pearl and Hermes Reef must be carefully sequestered to avoid contamination of gear bound for other remote islands. Special care must be taken to avoid contaminating gear storage areas and quarters aboard transporting vessels with seeds or insects from these islands.

General Rules:

- Regardless of origin or destination, inspect and clean all equipment, supplies, immediately prior to any trip to the Refuge. Carefully clean all clothing, footwear and soft gear following use to minimize risk of cross contamination of materials between islands.

- Pack supplies in plastic buckets with fitted lids or other sealable metal or plastic containers so they can be thoroughly cleaned inside and out. **Cardboard is not permitted on islands.** Cardboard boxes disintegrate in a short time and harbor seeds, animals, etc., which cannot be easily found or removed. **Wood is not permitted unless sealed on all surfaces.**

  Wooden boxes can also harbor insects and seeds and, therefore, are only allowed if well constructed (tight fitting seams are required). All wood must be treated, and inside and outside surfaces must be painted or varnished to provide a smooth, cleanable finish that seals all holes.

- Freeze or tarp and fumigate then seal all equipment (clothes, books, tents) immediately prior to departure. Food and cooking items need not be fumigated but should be cleaned and frozen, if freezable. Cameras, binoculars, radios, and other electronic equipment must be thoroughly cleaned, including internal inspection whenever possible, but they do not need to be frozen or fumigated. Such equipment can only be packed in wooden crates if treated as in #2 above. Any containers must contain new, clean packing materials and be frozen or fumigated.

- At present, Tern Island is the singular exception to the above rule having less stringent rules due to the large number of previously established invasive species. Careful inspection of all materials and containers is still required. However, it is acceptable to use wooden and cardboard containers for transporting supplies to Tem Island. In addition, there is no requirement for freezing or fumigating items disembarked at Tem. Although requirements for Tem Island are more lax, the Refuge is still concerned about the possibilities of new introductions.

Additional Special Conditions for Restricted Access to Nihoa Island:

Nihoa is one of the most pristine locations in the Refuge Complex. It is also inhabited by the highest number of federally listed endangered species. It is a small rugged island with many inaccessible areas. Introduction of any invasive species could have immediate, disastrous effects to natural resources. It would be almost impossible to mount any kind of control or eradication program on this island should an invasive species become established. Because of these reasons, access to Nihoa is strictly limited and rules governing entry are more stringent.

- Access to Nihoa by permittees would only be allowed under the direct supervision of a Refuge representative. The person, who shall be appointed by the Refuge Manager, would work with permittees to assure careful adherence with all rules for inspection, handling, and preparation of equipment. The Refuge Representative would have the authority to control and limit access to various parts of the island to protect animals, plants (especially endangered species), and archaeological sites. The Refuge Representative would have the authority to revoke access to the island or order an immediate departure from the island if conditions for working on the island are not fully met or are violated in some way.

- All field equipment made out of fabric material or wood must be new and never previously used in the Northwestern or main Hawaiian Islands. Equipment previously purchased or made for use on Nihoa that has been carefully sealed and stored while away from Nihoa, and not used elsewhere, may also be brought onto the island. Rules for freezing and/or fumigating are as described for other sites in the Refuge (see above).

- Clothing and personal effects must be cleaned and thoroughly inspected. All footwear (shoes, slippers, socks, etc.) must be new, unused, or previously only used on Nihoa and carefully sealed and stored while off of the island.

Rules Regarding Food:

Fresh foods that are typically transported to island field camps (potatoes, onions, cabbage, apples, oranges, etc.) are not likely to become established and flourish on the Refuge Complex and are allowed. However, other food items such as tomatoes could easily become established. Soil can contain many seeds, eggs, larvae, etc., and cannot be transported to or among islands.

Other food species such as alfalfa, mustard and cress, commonly used for sprouted greens, could potentially become established and cannot be brought to the islands. Other species such as mung beans, soybeans, and radishes would not likely survive on the islands and can be used for fresh greens. A list of fresh foods and seeds that are prohibited is provided below. Permittees should contact the Refuge Manager for more information or for questions about items not included on this list.

Strictly Prohibited:

Tomatoes (any variety), ray sunflower seeds, alfalfa seeds, mustard seeds.

Bulk dried fruits are allowed but should be frozen solid for at least one day to kill any insects.

Appendix E

Plan Implementation and Costs

Introduction

Following public review and comment on the Draft EA, public notification of the Service's decision, and CCP approval, Refuge staff would begin to implement the CCP. This appendix describes the various partnerships, management plans, staffing and projects required to implement the plan over the next 15 years.

Partnerships

Partnerships are an important component of implementation of the Jarvis Island NWR CCP. Refuge staff would strengthen existing partnerships with the U.S. Coast Guard, the National Oceanic and Atmospheric Administration, and the University of Hawaii Undersea Research Laboratory to implement enhanced law enforcement coverage at this remote location and facilitate inventory and monitoring of marine resources. In addition, the refuge staff would seek to enhance its volunteer program. Volunteers are critically important in providing the logistical support in the Honolulu office and field support required to effectively manage and operate year-round field camps at remote locations.

Step-Down Management Plans

The CCP is one of several plans necessary for refuge management. The CCP provides guidance in the form of goals, objectives, and strategies for several refuge program areas but may lack some of the specifics need for implementation. Given the abbreviated and qualitative once-a-year management activities identified in the preferred alternative, step-down plans would not be developed for individual program areas after CCP completion. The Draft Seabird Monitoring Assessment for Hawaii and the Pacific Islands (Citta and Reynolds, 2006), U.S. Pacific Islands Regional Shorebird Conservation Plan, Seabird Conservation Plan for the Pacific Region, and U.S. Coral Reef Task Force planning efforts would be applied to refuge operations described in the preferred alternative.

Staffing

The proportion of current staffing and proposed staffing within the Pacific Remote Islands NWR Complex dedicated to Jarvis are shown in the following tables. The proposed staffing indicates a 0.16 full-time-equivalent increase over current levels. This represents the difference in staffing needs from visiting Jarvis once every other year to once every year.

Current Staffing for Jarvis Island NWR

Staff	Employment Status and Proportion of Time[1]	Salary Rating
Project Leader	PFT (0.01 FTE)	GS 13
Supervisory Wildlife Biologist	PFT (0.07 FTE)	GS 12
Coral Reef Biologist	PFT (0.07 FTE)	GS 12
Administrative Officer	PFT (0.01 FTE)	GS 9

[1] PFT = Permanent Full Time; FTE = Full Time Equivalent where 1.0 equals one staff year.

Proposed Staffing for Jarvis Island NWR

Staff	Employment Status and Proportion of Time[1]	Salary Rating
Project Leader	PFT (0.02 FTE)	GS 13
Supervisory Wildlife Biologist	PFT (0.14 FTE)	GS 12
Coral Reef Biologist	PFT (0.14 FTE)	GS 12
Administrative Officer	PFT (0.02 FTE)	GS 9

[1] PFT = Permanent Full Time; FTE = Full Time Equivalent where 1.0 equals one staff year.

Projects

The table below contains projects developed as part of the Refuge Operating Needs System (RONS) and Service Asset Maintenance Management System (SAMMS). Brief project descriptions and their associated costs are provided. Funding of these projects would assist refuge staff in achieving the goals, objectives, and strategies of the CCP for Jarvis Island NWR.

Projects: RONS and SAMMS List

Project No.	Title and Description	Cost Estimate (Thousands)	Station Rank
97003	**Inventory and Monitor Terrestrial Resources:** Provide a wildlife biologist to inventory and monitor terrestrial plants, invertebrates and nesting seabirds. Remote Pacific Islands provide the only secure habitat for nesting seabirds, sea turtles and marine life within thousands of square miles of ocean.	325.25	9
00001	**Eliminate Exotic Rodent Species on Remote Pacific Islands:** Provide biological technicians and transportation expenses to restore habitat for pelagic seabirds and	194.0	10

Project No.	Title and Description	Cost Estimate (Thousands)	Station Rank
	terrestrial plant and animal species on Howland, Baker and Jarvis NWRs.		
980002	**Eliminate Exotic Rodent Species on Remote Pacific Islands:** Provide Wildlife Refuge Specialist to supervise biological technicians and transportation expenses to restore habitat for pelagic seabirds and terrestrial plant and animal species on Howland, Baker and Jarvis NWRs.	174.75	10
00002	**Develop interpretative program, Remote Island NWRs:** Develop a brochure for Howland, Baker, and Jarvis Island NWRs and host 3 special outreach events every year in Hawaii.	23.9	999
00006	**Staff and maintain a new vessel to accomplish basic refuge operations:** This vessel would provide basic logistical support for 16 islands and remote field stations on nine different national wildlife refuges across the Pacific Ocean. The vessel would be similar in size and capability to the M/V Tiglax at the Alaska Maritime NWR	204.8	3
00018	**Inventory and monitor coral reef resources:** Remote refuges contain some of the most valuable and spectacular marine and coralline resources in the National Wildlife Refuge System. Jarvis Island NWR is so remote that basic knowledge of marine resources is lacking. There is a need to perform biennial monitoring of the marine resources at this refuge.	137.0	4
98004	**Install remote surveillance system:** Acquire camera equipment and service contract with a satellite communications provider to detect incursion by unauthorized visitors, such as poachers and commercial fishing vessels to assist the Coast Guard and Refuge Law Enforcement Officers in investigating illegal activities within the Refuge.	241.2	14
90100411	**Replace broken, rotten, and vandalized signs:** Replace degraded entrance signs to deter trespass and prevent introduction of invasive species.	190.0	6

This page left intentionally blank.

Appendix F

Wilderness Review for Jarvis Island NWR

I. General Information on Wilderness Reviews

Wilderness review is the process used to determine whether or not to recommend lands or waters in the National Wildlife Refuge System (System) to the United States Congress (Congress) for designation as wilderness. Planning policy for the System (602 FW 3) mandates conducting wilderness reviews every 15 years through the Comprehensive Conservation Planning (CCP) process.

The wilderness review process has three phases: inventory, study, and recommendation. After first identifying lands and waters that meet the minimum criteria for wilderness, the resulting wilderness study areas (WSA) are further evaluated to determine if they merit recommendation from the Service to the Secretary of Interior for inclusion in the National Wilderness Preservation System (NWPS). Areas recommended for designation are managed to maintain wilderness character in accordance with management goals, objectives, and strategies outlined in the final CCP until Congress makes a decision or the CCP is amended to modify or remove the wilderness proposal. A brief discussion of wilderness inventory, study, and recommendation follows.

Wilderness Inventory
The wilderness inventory consists of identifying areas that minimally meet the requirements for of wilderness as defined in the Wilderness Act of 1964 (Wilderness Act). Wilderness is defined as an area which:

- Has at least five thousand acres of land or is of sufficient size as to make practicable its preservation and use in an unimpaired condition, or be capable of restoration to wilderness character through appropriate management at the time of review, or be a roadless island;
- Generally appears to have been affected primarily by the forces of nature, with the imprint of man's work substantially unnoticeable;
- Has outstanding opportunities for solitude or a primitive and unconfined type of recreation; and
- May also contain ecological, geological, or other features of scientific, educational, scenic, or historical value. These features and values, though desirable, are not necessary for an area to qualify as a wilderness.

Wilderness Study
During the study phase, lands and waters qualifying for wilderness as a result of the inventory are studied to analyze values (ecological, recreational, cultural, spiritual), resources (*e.g.,* wildlife, water, vegetation, minerals, soils), and uses (habitat management, public use) within the area. The findings of the study help determine whether to recommend the area for designation as wilderness.

Wilderness Recommendation

Once a wilderness study determines that a WSA meets the requirements for inclusion in the NWPS, a wilderness study report that presents the results of the wilderness review, accompanied by a Legislative Environmental Impact Statement (LEIS), is prepared. The wilderness study report and LEIS that support wilderness designation are then transmitted through the Secretary of Interior to the President of United States, and ultimately to the United States Congress for approval.

The following sections summarize the inventory and study phases of the wilderness review for Jarvis.

II. Wilderness Inventory

The wilderness inventory is a broad look at the planning area to identify WSAs. These WSAs are roadless areas within refuge boundaries, including submerged lands and their associated water column, that meet the minimum criteria for wilderness identified in Sect. 2. (c) of the Wilderness Act. A WSA must meet the minimum size criteria (or be a roadless island), appear natural, and provide outstanding opportunities for solitude or primitive recreation. Other supplemental values are evaluated, but not required. In order to identify WSAs, Jarvis was divided into two inventory units based upon the differences between the terrestrial and marine ecological resources. Inventory Unit A is the 648-acre roadless island known as Jarvis Island, and Inventory Unit B is composed of the 34,319 combined acres of coral reefs, submergent lands and their associated water column lying within 3 nmi from the shoreline at the mean high water mark of Jarvis Island. The inventory of roadless areas, submerged lands, and associated water column of Jarvis and application of the wilderness criteria is described in the following sections and summarized in Table F-1.

Evaluation of Size Criteria for Roadless Areas, Roadless Islands, and Submergent Lands and Associated Water Column

Identification of roadless areas, roadless islands, and submerged lands and associated water column, required gathering land status maps, land use and road inventory data, satellite imagery, aerial photographs, and personal observations of areas within refuge boundaries. "Roadless" refers to the absence of improved roads suitable and maintained for public travel by means of motorized vehicles primarily intended for highway use. Wilderness inventory units currently owned by the Service in fee title were evaluated. These units include Jarvis Island and the submergent lands and waters lying within 3 nmi of shore.

Inventory units meet the size criteria for a WSA if any one of the following standards applies.

- An area with over 5,000 contiguous acres. State and private lands are not included in making this acreage determination.
- A roadless island of any size. A roadless island is defined as an area surrounded by permanent waters or that is markedly distinguished from the surrounding lands by topographical or ecological features.

- An area of less than 5,000 contiguous Federal acres that is of sufficient size as to make practicable its preservation and use in an unimpaired condition, and of a size suitable for wilderness management.
- An area of less than 5,000 contiguous Federal acres that is contiguous with a designated wilderness, recommended wilderness, or area under wilderness review by another Federal wilderness managing agency such as the Forest Service, National Park Service, or Bureau of Land Management.

There are no roads on Jarvis Island, and the submerged lands and associated water column meet the minimum acreage criteria, thus both inventory units within the refuge boundary meet one or more of the size criteria for wilderness study areas. The physical features of these units are described in detail in the Draft Jarvis CCP/EA, Chapter 3.

Evaluation of the Naturalness Criteria
A WSA must meet the naturalness criteria. Section 2.(c) of the Wilderness Act defines wilderness as an area that "…generally appears to have been affected primarily by the forces of nature with the imprint of man's work substantially unnoticeable." The area must appear natural to the average visitor rather than "pristine." The presence of ecologically accurate, historic landscape conditions is not required. An area may include some man-made features and human impacts provided they are substantially unnoticeable in the unit as a whole. Human-caused hazards, such as the presence of unexploded ordnance from military activity, and the physical impacts of refuge management facilities and activities are also considered in the evaluation of the naturalness criteria. An area may not be considered unnatural in appearance solely on the basis of "sights and sounds" of human impacts and activities outside the boundary of the unit. The cumulative effects of these factors were considered in the evaluation of naturalness for each wilderness inventory unit.

In the wilderness inventory, specific man-made features and other human impacts need to be identified that affect the overall apparent naturalness of the tract. Based upon the Preferred Alternative contained in the draft CCP/EA, the following factors were primary considerations in evaluating the naturalness of the inventory units:

Historical
- abandoned crushed coral roadways;
- Jarvis Light daybeacon (aid to navigation);
- Colonizing era ruins
- Shipwreck remains of *Amaranth*
- *Amaranth* memorial cairn
- abandoned guano mine tailing piles.

Little can be seen of the historical artifacts found on Jarvis. Wind erosion, past storms and vegetative growth have muted any visual impact of these cultural sites. Consequently, they are indistinguishable from adjacent habitats on the island. Most other artifacts equally blend into the environment. The Jarvis Light daybeacon, some rock walls, and the cairn are the only visual intrusions into an otherwise natural setting.

Management Activities:
- refuge boundary sign;
- field camp;
- generators;
- invasive species control;
- collect and stockpile marine debris;
- migratory bird surveys;
- marine surveys (including SCUBA); and
- boat transportation.

A 4' x 8' boundary sign announcing the name and ownership of the island is maintained on Jarvis. The sign is informational in nature, identifying the sanctuary status the island enjoys. The primary management intrusion to the naturalness of Jarvis is during the deployment and demobilization of field camps. Transportation from Honolulu, Hawaii across 1,263 nmi of open ocean to Jarvis is only safely and reliably possible with motorized ocean-going marine vessels. Once the marine transport vessel arrives at Jarvis, small boats with outboard motors are deployed to transport two biologists and their field camp gear to the island. Once on the island, biologists set up tents, sleeping gear, food, and other supplies. Walking surveys occur across the island to document bird species presence, potentially hand pull or hand spray invasive plant species, inventory cultural sites, and collect and stockpile marine debris. Marine surveys also occur. They are based from the marine vessel primarily using SCUBA. Field camps are planned to last for 2 days and typically occur once every two years. Occasional field camps with 5-8 individuals staying for up to 2 weeks have occurred in the past. During these extended field camps, diesel-powered generators have been used to operate communication equipment. All other mechanical equipment such as air compressors for SCUBA equipment remain on the marine transport vessel. Upon demobilization of the field camp, all equipment and debris are removed. An indirect human impact to the naturalness of Jarvis is the presence of marine debris that washes onto coral reefs and beaches. Attempts to remove and stockpile this debris for eventual removal occur during field camps. Otherwise, Jarvis is an isolated, uninhabited island in the middle of the Pacific ocean for the vast majority of time.

Both Jarvis inventory units meet the naturalness criteria. Overall, the forces of nature sculpt the island's resources. Wave action erodes and accretes shorelines and rearranges underwater coral features. Rainfall patterns either suppress or encourage vegetative growth with brown and barren ground during drought and lush grasses and forbs during wet periods. Bird life is the dominant feature with nesting seabirds common throughout the year. Occasional field camps infrequently intrude on this isolation.

Although historic markers, monuments, and other signs of past human occupation exist, they do not detract from Howland meeting the naturalness criteria since they are a minor component of the landscape and are substantially unnoticeable in the area as a whole. The submerged lands, with the exception of scattered marine debris also meet the naturalness criteria.

Evaluation of Outstanding Opportunities for Solitude or Primitive and Unconfined Recreation
In addition to meeting the size and naturalness criteria, a WSA must provide outstanding opportunities for solitude or primitive recreation. The area does not have to possess outstanding

opportunities for both solitude and primitive and unconfined recreation, and does not need to have outstanding opportunities on every acre. Further, an area does not have to be open to public use and access to qualify under these criteria. Congress has designated a number of wilderness areas in the NWPS that are closed to public access to protect ecological resource values.

Opportunities for solitude refers to the ability of a visitor to be alone and secluded from other visitors in the area. Primitive and unconfined recreation means non-motorized, dispersed outdoor recreation activities that do not require developed facilities or mechanical transport. These primitive recreation activities may provide opportunities to experience challenge and risk, self reliance, and adventure.

These two opportunity "elements" are not well defined by the Wilderness Act but in most cases can be expected to occur together. However, an outstanding opportunity for solitude may be present in an area offering only limited primitive recreation potential. Conversely, an area may be so attractive for recreation use that experiencing solitude is not an option.

The following factors and their cumulative effects were the primary considerations in evaluating the availability of outstanding opportunities for solitude or primitive unconfined recreation at Jarvis:
- island size, vegetation, and terrain;
- distance to habitation, whether mainland or an inhabited island;
- presence of operating lighthouse or aid to navigation and associated structures; and
- view shed within and from refuge boundary.

Solitude is the overwhelming force that visitors experience on Jarvis. The island is separated by over 1,263 nautical miles from Hawaii, and approximately 184 nmi from Kiritimatai Island Atoll, the nearest inhabited island. Expanses of open ocean with no other landform are visible from every angle. The island itself, with the exception of a few historical features, is a mixture of short grass and shrubs, bare ground, and shoreline beaches and cobble. In the past, field camps have been temporary, with only 2 individuals spending 2 days every 2 years. However, the Preferred Alternative in the Draft Jarvis CCP/EA proposes to visit the refuge every year with the same number of individuals for the same duration. Underwater, coral reefs are pristine and the open-water depths are devoid of human presence.

Since establishment, Jarvis has been and will remain closed to general public access in order to protect the valuable seabird and marine resource values. Thus, there are no outdoor recreational opportunities.

Both Jarvis inventory units meet the solitude criteria, but do not meet the primitive unconfined recreation criteria.

Evaluation of Supplemental Values
Supplemental values are defined by the Wilderness Act as "ecological, geological, or other features of scientific, educational, scenic, or historic value." Jarvis Island and its surrounding coral reefs and deep water areas compose a complete and functioning ecosystem. Isolated, predator-free islands are valuable and often required for successful seabird nesting. Nearshore

waters, coral reefs, and associated currents combine and provide food resources for foraging seabirds and coral reef communities. The position and underwater gradient of Jarvis in deep ocean currents allows these currents to reach the surface, thereby increasing rates of productivity for plants, corals and vertebrate species. These rich ecological resources in a relatively pristine and unaltered environment provide unique opportunities for scientific study and environmental education. There are no known archaeological resources on Jarvis. Historically, Jarvis Island was important to early colonization efforts during the guano mining era. Historical artifacts such as isolated building ruins, a memorial cairn and plaque commemorating the *Amaranth* grounding, and guano mining excavations are present but eroded, covered by vegetation, and otherwise assimilated into the environment and indistinguishable from the natural environment. One landmark, the Jarvis Light day beacon, contrasts vividly with the overall expansive vistas of open ocean and island habitats. These values are not required for wilderness but their presence compliments the requirements for wilderness designation. Please see Chapter 3 of the Draft CCP/EA for a more complete description of these supplemental values.

Inventory Findings and Wilderness Study Areas

Both inventory units meet the minimum criteria for consideration as WSAs (Figure F-1). These two units are either roadless islands or meet minimum size requirements, are primarily natural, and meet the solitude or unconfined recreation criteria. The units are identified as:

- WSA-A: Jarvis Island WSA, and
- WSA-B: Coral reefs, submergent lands, and associated water column of the Jarvis Island WSA.

Figure F-1. Wilderness Study Areas

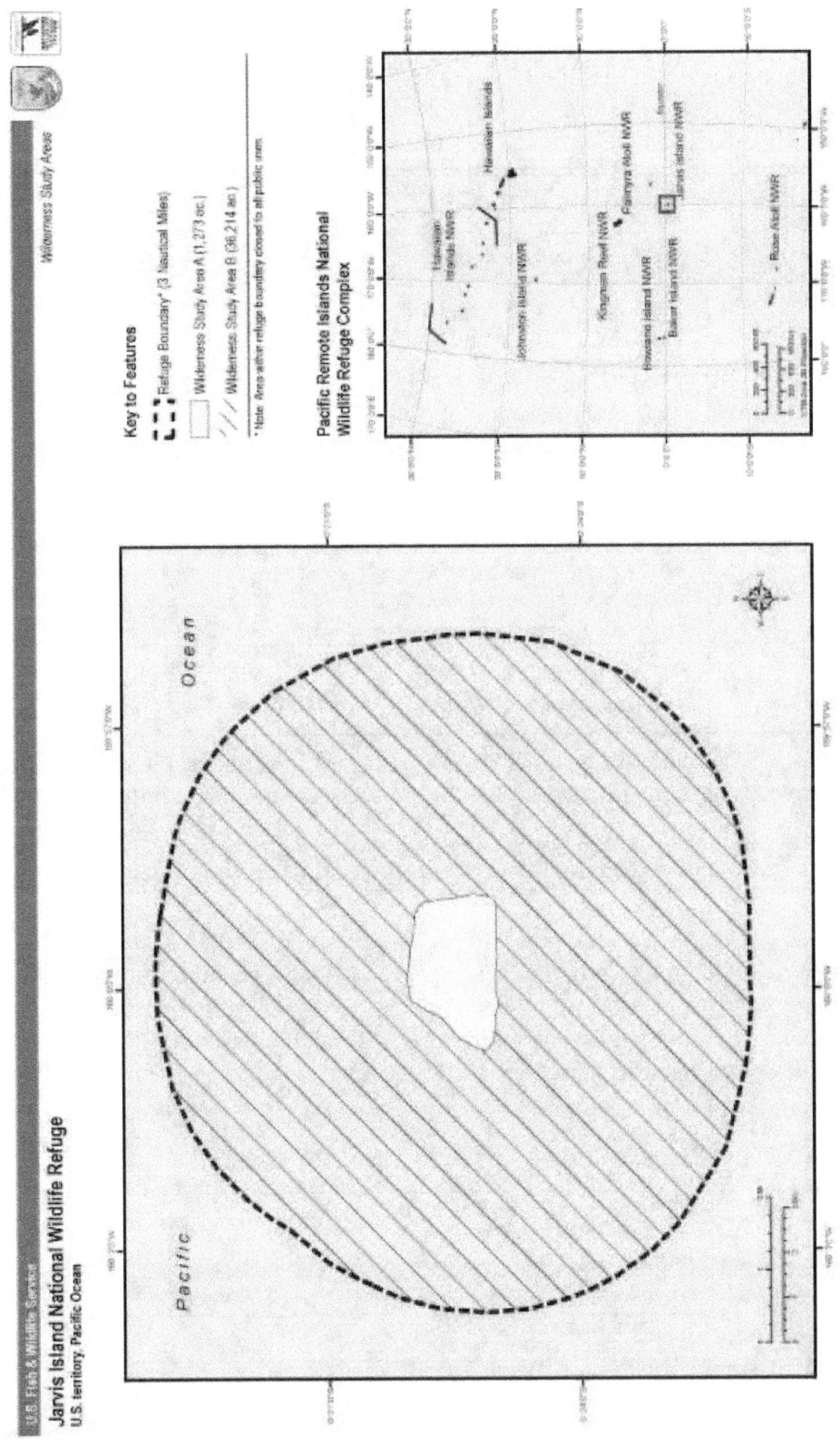

Table F-1 Wilderness Inventory Summary

	Inventory Unit A: Jarvis Island (1,273 acres)	Inventory Unit B: Submerged lands and waters to 3 nmi (36,214 acres)
Required Components		
(1) Has at least 5000 acres of land or is of sufficient size to make practicable its preservation and use in an unconfined condition, or is a roadless island.	Yes. Is a roadless island.	Yes. Approximately 36,214 acres contained within the territorial sea from mean high tide to 3 nmi.
(2) Generally appears to have been affected primarily by the forces of nature, with the imprint of man's work substantially unnoticeable.	Yes. Not diminished by day beacon and other artifacts.	Yes. Coral reefs and other underwater features untouched by humans.
(3a) Has outstanding opportunities for solitude.	Yes. Uninhabited island 1000 nmi from Hawaii.	Yes. Isolation from habitation both on surface and below.
(3b) Has outstanding opportunities for a primitive and unconfined type of recreation.	No. Refuge is closed to all recreational activities.	No. Refuge is closed to all recreational activities.
Other Components		
(4) Contains ecological, geological or other features of scientific, educational, scenic, or historical value.	Jarvis Light day beacon, *Amaranth* memorial, guano mining, colonization ruins, historic shipwreck, and nesting seabirds.	Pristine coral reefs and associated marine fish, mammals, and turtles abound.
Summary		
Parcel qualifies as a wilderness study area (meets criteria 1, 2 & 3a or 3b).	Yes	Yes

III. Wilderness Study

The two WSAs identified in the Wilderness Inventory were further evaluated to determine suitability for designation, management, and preservation as wilderness. Considerations in this evaluation included:

- quality of wilderness values; and,
- capability for management of refuge as wilderness (or manageability) and minimum requirements/tools analysis.

This information provides a basis to compare the impacts of a range of management alternatives and determine the most appropriate management direction for each WSA.

Evaluation of Wilderness Values
The following information considers the quality of the WSAs' mandatory and supplemental wilderness characteristics.

Size
Both WSA-A and WSA-B meet the minimum size criteria being a 1,273-acre roadless island and a 36,214-acre marine ecosystem respectively.

Naturalness
Both of the WSAs generally appear to have been affected primarily by the forces of nature, with the imprint of human uses and activities substantially unnoticeable. Except for the footprint of the long-abandoned airstrip and the few small features mentioned in the Wilderness Inventory, all emergent and submerged features were entirely created by the natural processes of volcanism; wind erosion; wave erosion; water erosion; seabird deposits; vegetation deposits; geological subsidence; and reef growth and consolidation from coral, coralline algae, and giant clam calcification during the past 50 to 80 million years. No substantial features were constructed or modified by humans during the island's entire geological history. The impacts of past human presence are small in terms of constructed features (beacons), and are barely apparent (ground-level views of mining pits and a boat channel), or transitory (marine debris that washes up or blows in from the surrounding sea and air). A few remnant, rusty fuel drums is the only trash feature that is not transient, but its overall impact to naturalness is minimal. See Chapter 3 of the Draft Jarvis CCP/EA for a more detailed description of natural and cultural features. Management activities will temporarily disturb the naturalness of the area. Field camps lasting for 2 days will be visible across the island. Occasional use of generators will produce noise. However, modern generators produce decibel levels lower than speaking voice levels. Transportation by motorized marine vessel, the only safe, practical and reliable means available to arrive on the island, is equally temporary.

Outstanding Opportunities for Solitude and Primitive Recreation
Both of the WSAs offer outstanding opportunities for solitude.

Solitude overwhelms the human spirit at Jarvis. The only noise on the island is from pounding surf, winds, buzzing insects, and the calls of birds. Underwater, all that is heard is one's own breath, the surf, and the sound of fish feeding on coral. The blue of the sky and sea and the brightness of the stark landscape saturate the visual character; and birds, winds, and surf saturate the acoustic character of the refuge. It is hard to image a more remote, isolated, and truly more wilderness experience in the entire equatorial Pacific than when standing on the island or diving on adjacent reefs.

There are no permanent improvements of any kind to accommodate visitors reaching the island. The capacity to reach Jarvis without substantial investment, preplanning, and permission is considerable and further restricts the capability of individuals from reaching the island and intruding on the opportunity for solitude. The island itself is inaccessible except by small craft lightered from a transport ship during calm seas. There are no human inhabitants on Jarvis. The nearest humans live 330 nmi to the southeast where less than 5,000 Kiribati people inhabit Kiritimatai Atoll. There are no other inhabitants elsewhere in the Line Islands. These logistical constraints contribute to the maintenance of solitude.

Supplemental Values

Both of the WSAs offer outstanding ecological values with features of scientific, educational, scenic interest, and historical value. Pristine coral reefs, reef fish, giant clams, beaches, native terrestrial vegetation, unexplored deep slopes, localized upwelling currents, migratory shorebirds, and large populations and variety of seabirds are among the strong ecological values. The lack of historic and current human impact provides a rare opportunity to study unaltered marine ecosystems, and the impact that global climate change may have on these systems. The sheer vastness of the ocean landscape, punctuated by a small dot of land, and the multitude of bird and marine life attracted to it, provide a sense of awe and spectacular beauty to the landscape. The remaining features of early colonization efforts stand testament to the bravery of those early pioneers, and the ability of nature to endure.

Evaluation of Manageability and Minimum Requirements/Tools Analysis

Originally administered by the U.S. Department of Interior's Office of Territorial Affairs, the Secretary of the Interior (Secretary), on June 27, 1974, designated Jarvis Island and its territorial sea extending to the 3 nautical mile (nmi) limit as a unit of the System (39 FR 27930). The U.S. Fish and Wildlife Service administers all units of the system pursuant to the Administration Act. The acquisition authority for establishing the refuge is found in the Fish and Wildlife Act of 1956 (16 U.S.C. 742f(b)(1)). It states the general purpose for establishing the refuge is "... for the development, advancement, management, conservation, and protection of fish and wildlife resources ...", and "... for the benefit of the United States Fish and Wildlife Service, in performing its activities and services" (16 U.S.C. 742f (a) (4)). The specific purpose for establishing Jarvis is (USFWS 1973 "...the preservation of the complete ecosystem, terrestrial as well as marine. Special emphasis to be given to the large seabird nesting colonies."

There are no valid existing private rights, including mineral rights, associated with any of these WSAs.

Several management activities are required for the Service to meet responsibilities for managing Jarvis Island and its associated marine waters as a national wildlife refuge as specified in relevant legislation and policies. A complete description of management activities can be found in Chapter 2 of the Draft Jarvis CCP/EA. The following is a brief description of management activities as they relate to minimum requirement determinations of activities occurring within designated wilderness.

Section 4(c) of the Wilderness Act of 1964 lists several generally prohibited uses including no temporary roads, no use of motor vehicles, no motorized equipment or motorboats, no aircraft landings, no other forms of mechanical transport, and no structure or installation. However, Section 4(c) also states an exception to these general prohibitions: "...as necessary to meet minimum requirements for the administration of the area for the purpose of this Act..." Examples of actions that may satisfy this exception include recreational developments such as trails, bridges, and signs.

Each WSA on Jarvis can be managed to preserve its wilderness character in perpetuity, recognizing that using a "minimum requirements" approach would be required for all activities. Existing refuge management activities within the WSAs are consistent with management direction in the Wilderness Act and current Service wilderness stewardship policy in the Refuge Manual (6 RM 8). These management activities include: motorized marine vessel transportation to and from Jarvis; establishing temporary field camps (typically 2 days every other year); small motorboat operations used in deployment and demobilization of field camp operations; survey and monitoring of habitat, seabird and other wildlife monitoring activities; control of invasive species using hand pulling or hand spraying; use of solar powered electronic calling devices to encourage nesting by extirpated seabird species; use of portable generators and solar power to operate communications and other equipment; and monitoring the marine ecosystem with the use of SCUBA equipment. None of the current or expected refuge management activities would permanently diminish the wilderness character of Jarvis. Additionally, there are no plans to construct permanent facilities or structures to accommodate these uses or activities.

Located in the central Pacific Ocean, transportation to Jarvis can only occur with the use of ocean-going marine vessels. The only practical and safe mode of vessel propulsion is gas or diesel powered engine. While it is possible to use sail power to navigate to the island, the reliability of mechanical engines provides a margin of safety to escape extreme weather hazards, or proceed on course and on time in the absence of wind. For the same reasons of safety and practicality, small motorized vessels are used to transport equipment and personnel from the transport vessel to the island to establish field camps and conduct biological survey and monitoring activities. Rough surf, shallow coral reefs, and strong winds and ocean currents preclude the use of non-motorized craft to safely navigate these hazards.

Field camps themselves are temporary, consisting of tents, portable tables, chairs, cooking gear, and scientific equipment. Most field camps are set up for a period of 1 to 2 days. No permanent structures are established, and no motorized equipment is used to transport equipment around the island. Field camp activities consist of monitoring habitat and nesting seabird populations, inventorying the condition of known historic resources, and collecting and stockpiling of marine debris. Portable diesel powered generators are components of field camp equipment and are typically used to operate two-way radio communication equipment.

Wildlife managers often use electronic calling devices to attract nesting seabird species to suitable nesting locations. Powered by small solar panels, these devices can be placed in inconspicuous locations and produce only sounds that occur naturally on the island. Once a species is attracted to the island, the calling device can then be removed. Monitoring of the marine ecosystem occurs from scientists based aboard the marine transportation vessel. Small motorboats often provide safe transportation to specific research sites near Howland. SCUBA equipment is often used to complete marine surveys and is the only safe and practical method of conducting underwater marine surveys.

In summary, safety, practicality, and effectiveness require the occasional use of management programs and associated tools (some of which are generally prohibited by the Wilderness Act) to pursue achievement of refuge purposes, goals and objectives. Current and proposed refuge management would be consistent with wilderness designation and management of both WSAs. Although occasionally diminished, none of the resource values identified above would be permanently impacted because of wilderness designation and the management described herein.

IV. Development of Alternatives

After evaluating the quality of wilderness values, manageability, minimum management requirements, the following alternatives were developed and analyzed for wilderness designation.

Alternative A (No Action).
Under this alternative, no WSAs would be recommended as suitable for wilderness designation. The refuge lands and waters would be managed as they have been in the past to accomplish refuge purposes in accordance with legal and policy guidance for the System.

Alternative B
Only the emergent lands, WSA-A, would be recommended for inclusion in the National Wilderness Preservation System.

Alternative C
Both WSA-A and WSA-B, which includes the emergent lands and the submerged lands and associated water column would be immediately recommended for inclusion in the National Wilderness Preservation System (NWPS). Selection of this alternative would require the completion of an EIS.

Alternative D (Preferred Alternative)
Both WSA-A and WSA-B, which includes the emergent lands and the submerged lands and associated water column of Jarvis would be recommended for inclusion in the NWPS. Both wilderness study areas would be managed to ensure their wilderness character was not adversely impacted. However, the recommendation to include these areas in the NWPS would be postponed until such time that CCPs and their associated wilderness inventories and studies for remote Pacific Island NWRs were completed. At such a time, a wilderness study report and associated Legislative Environmental Impact Statement that

encompasses remote Pacific Island refuges would be prepared. Alternative D is identified here as the Preferred Alternative for the Wilderness Review of Jarvis, and is a component of the Preferred Alternative in the Draft Jarvis CCP/EA.

Alternatives considered but eliminated from detailed study
Federal agencies are required by NEPA to rigorously explore and objectively evaluate all reasonable alternatives and to briefly discuss the reasons for eliminating any alternatives that were not developed in detail (40 CFR 1502.14). It was determined that there was no benefit in analyzing partial wilderness alternatives. There are no feasible or practical boundary adjustments that would improve the manageability of an individual WSA.

This page left intentionally blank.

Appendix G

STATEMENT OF COMPLIANCE
for Implementation of the
Jarvis Island National Wildlife Refuge
Comprehensive Conservation Plan

The following executive orders and legislative acts have been reviewed as they apply to implementation of the Comprehensive Conservation Plan (CCP) for the Jarvis Island National Wildlife Refuge (Jarvis).

National Environmental Policy Act (1969) (42 U.S.C. 4321 et seq.). The CCP planning process is conducted in accordance with National Environmental Policy Act implementing procedures, Department of Interior and Service procedures, and is performed in coordination with the affected public. Procedures used to reach this decision meet the requirements of the National Environmental Policy Act and its implementing regulations in 40 CFR Parts 1500-1508. These procedures include: the development of a range of alternatives for the Jarvis CCP; analysis of the likely effects of each alternative; and public involvement throughout the planning process.

The CCP management objectives and alternatives are integrated into an environmental assessment document and process, including the release of a draft CCP/EA for a 30-day public comment period. Public notices of availability of the draft CCP/EA include a Federal Register notice, news releases to local media outlets, the Service's refuge planning website, and planning updates. Copies of the CCP/EA and planning updates were distributed to an extensive mailing list. In addition, the Service met with staff from the Hawaii Department of Land and Natural Resources and the National Oceanic and Atmospheric Administration. Revisions to the Final CCP are based on public comments received from the draft CCP/EA. Comment letters and Service response to comments can be found as an Appendix in the Final CCP.

National Historic Preservation Act (1966) (16 U.S. C.470 et seq.). This act requires Federal agencies to consult with the President's Advisory Council on Historic Preservation (ACHP), State or Territorial Historic Preservation Officers, and the National Park Service (NPS) for any proposed actions that may affect cultural resources eligible for the National Register of Historic Places. Consultation has occurred with the ACHP and NPS for their input. Consultation with a State Historic Preservation Officer is not required for this proposal because Jarvis lies outside any state jurisdiction. No Territorial Historic Preservation Officer is assigned to Jarvis. Rather territories/possessions lie in the jurisdiction of the Advisory Council on Historic Preservation (ACHP).

The management of archaeological and cultural resources of Jarvis complies with the regulations of Section 106 of the National Historic Preservation Act. No historic properties listed in or eligible for listing in the National Register of Historic Places have been identified on Jarvis. No historic properties are known to be affected by the proposed action based on the criteria of an effect or adverse effect as an undertaking defined in 36 CFR 800.9 and

Service Manual 614 FW 2. Determining whether a particular action has a potential to affect cultural resources is an ongoing process that occurs as step-down and site-specific project plans are developed. Should historic properties be identified in the future, the Service will comply with the National Historic Preservation Act if any management actions have the potential to affect any these properties.

Comprehensive Environmental Response, Compensation, and Liability Act (CERCLA), Secretarial Order 3127, and Section 211 of the Superfund Amendments and Reauthorization Act (SARA) of 1986 (10 U.S.C. 2701-2706, 2810-2811). Contamination resulting from military occupation is required to be mitigated as a Formerly Used Defense Site (FUDS). Any FUDS is part of the Defense Environmental Restoration Program (DERP), administered by the Army Corps of Engineers (ACOE). The DERP is responsible for the identification, investigation, research and development, and cleanup of contamination from hazardous substances, and pollutants and contaminants; correction of environmental damage such as detection and disposal of unexploded ordnance; and demolition and removal of unsafe buildings and structures at former Department of Defense sites. In 1986, the ACOE completed their responsibilities under DERP. No contaminant or hazardous waste materials are currently known to exist on Jarvis.

Executive Order 13175. Consultation and Coordination with Indian Tribal Governments. As required under Secretary of the Interior Order 3206 American Indian Tribal Rights, Federal-Tribal Responsibilities, and the Endangered Species Act, the Refuge Manager determined that there are no tribal governments associated with Jarvis. Thus, there was no coordination with any American Indian tribe.

Executive Order 12372. Intergovernmental Review. Coordination and consultation with other affected Federal agencies has been completed through personal contact by Service planners, refuge managers, and supervisors. In addition, the refuge manager determined there are no local, state or tribal governments associated with Jarvis.

Executive Order 12898. Federal Actions to Address Environmental Justice in Minority and Low-Income Populations. All Federal actions must address and identify, as appropriate, disproportionately high and adverse human health or environmental effects of its programs, policies, and activities on minority populations, low-income populations, and Indian Tribes in the United States. The CCP was evaluated and no adverse human health or environmental effects were identified for minority or low-income populations, Indian Tribes, or anyone else.

Migratory Bird Treaty Act (MBTA)(16 U.S.C. 703-712) Jarvis is an important site for migratory shorebirds and nesting seabirds. Protecting nesting seabird habitat is the major purpose of the refuge, and is consistent with the provisions of MBTA. All of the proposed alternatives would be consistent with the refuge purpose and the MBTA in protecting of these birds, although the proposed action would afford more benefits. This planning effort is being coordinated with other offices of the Service and Interior that have responsibilities pertaining to the MBTA.

Executive Order 13186. Responsibilities of Federal Agencies to Protect Migratory Birds. This Order directs departments and agencies to take certain actions to further implement the Migratory Bird Treaty Act. A provision of the Order directs Federal agencies to consider the impacts of their activities, especially in reference to birds on the Fish and Wildlife Service's list of Birds of Conservation (Management) Concern (BCC). It also directs agencies to incorporate conservation recommendations and objectives found within the North American Waterbird Conservation Plan and bird conservation plans developed by Partners in Flight (PIF) into agency planning. Species selected as focal conservation targets in the CCP were identified from multiple sources including pertinent BCC lists, applicable Flyway Management Plans, and regional seabird and shorebird conservation plans. The effects of all alternatives on focal conservation targets were assessed during this planning process.

Endangered Species Act (ESA)(16 U.S.C. 1531-1544) The ESA provides for the conservation of threatened and endangered species of fish, wildlife, and plants by Federal action and by encouraging the establishment of state programs. It provides for the determination and listing of endangered and threatened species and the designation of critical habitats. Section 7 of the ESA requires refuge managers to perform consultation before initiating projects that affect or may affect endangered species.

Jarvis provides feeding and potential nesting habitat for two species of endangered sea turtle: the hawksbill turtle, *Eretmochelys imbricata* and the green turtle *Chelonia mydas*. In accordance with section 7 of the Endangered Species Act of 1973, as amended (16 U.S.C. 1531 et. Seq.), the Service, as a component of this CCP/EA, evaluated potential impacts to the two listed turtle species. It was determined that undertaking any action as part of any alternative in this CCP will have no affect on either of the two turtle species. Therefore, formal consultation with NOAA-NMFS is not required and will not be initiated.

National Wildlife Administration Act of 1966, as amended by The National Wildlife Refuge System Improvement Act of 1997 (16 U.S.C. 668dd-668ee). The National Wildlife Refuge System Improvement Act requires the Service to develop and implement a comprehensive conservation plan for each refuge. These conservation plans identify and describe a refuge purpose; refuge vision and goals; fish, wildlife, and plant populations and related habitats; archaeological and cultural values of the refuge; issues that may affect populations and habitats of fish, wildlife, and plants; actions necessary to restore and improve biological diversity of the refuge; and opportunities for wildlife-dependent recreation.

Wilderness Preservation Act of 1964 (Wilderness Act). The Wilderness Act requires the Service to evaluate the suitability of Jarvis for wilderness designation (Appendix F) and has found that both wilderness study areas meet wilderness criteria. Recommendation for Jarvis to be included in the Wilderness Preservation System is deferred until such time that other remote Pacific island refuges are evaluated for wilderness designation and a combined proposal as part of a larger comprehensive Legislative Environmental Impact Statement is prepared.

Magnuson-Stevens Fisheries Management and Conservation Act (16 U.S.C. 1801-1882)
This act provides the guidance for sustainable management of commercial fisheries in Federal waters by NOAA in consultation with Regional Fisheries Management Councils that develop fisheries management plans (FMPS) subject to NOAA approval, monitoring and implementation. The Western Pacific Regional Fisheries Management Council (WESPAC) and NOAA have implemented and approved several FMPS that apply to U.S. insular Pacific island waters. The FMPS were all implemented after Jarvis was established in 1974 and include plans for: 1) pelagic fish; 2) bottom fish including some reef species; 3) crustaceans including lobsters; and, 4) precious corals. Commercial activities including commercial fishing are prohibited in surrounding marine water and benthic habitat out to the 3 nmi limit because Jarvis Island is established as a no-take marine protected area and a National Wildlife Refuge. Moreover, the Service retains jurisdiction and management for any fisheries within the refuge. Available information indicates commercial fishing under the auspices of any of the FMPS is not being pursued outside the 3 nmi boundary of the refuge. Informal consultation also indicates that WESPAC continues to honor Service jurisdiction and authorities within the 3 nmi offshore boundary of the refuge (K. Simonds, per. comm. with J. Maragos 2006).

Executive Order 13089, Coral Reef Protection (June 11, 1998) The purpose of this Executive order is "...to preserve and protect the biodiversity, health, heritage, and social and economic value of U.S. coral reef ecosystems and the marine environment...." It directs all Federal agencies to identify actions that may affect U.S. coral reefs; utilize their programs and authorities to protect and enhance coral reef ecosystems; and assure their actions would not degrade those ecosystems. Federal agencies whose actions affect U.S. coral reef ecosystems are further directed to implement measures needed to research, monitor, manage, and restore affected ecosystems, including, but not limited to, measures reducing impacts from pollution, sedimentation, and fishing. This Executive Order also initially established the U.S. Coral Reef Task Force, co-chaired by the Secretaries of the Interior and Commerce, through the Administrator of NOAA. The Task Force has oversight responsibility for implementation of policy and Federal agency responsibilities found in this order, and support activities under the U.S. Coral Reef Initiative. In addition, this order directs the Task Force to work cooperatively with State, territory, commonwealth, and local government partners to map, monitor, conserve, mitigate, and restore coral reef ecosystems.

The Proposed Action and other alternatives are fully consistent with the spirit and intent of the Executive order. Copies of the Draft CCP/EA would be provided to the Directorate of the Coral Reef Task Force for coordination.

Coral Reef Conservation Act and Executive Order 13158, Marine Protected Areas (16 U.S.C. 6401-6409)(May 26, 2000). These statutes collectively direct Federal agencies to coordinate among themselves and State and Territorial governments via the Coral Reef Task Force to protect and enhance coral reefs and avoid actions that degrade reefs, promote marine protected area development and reef restoration, and provide conservation grants and cooperative agreements (including States and institutions) to conduct research and development of existing and candidate marine protected areas located on coral reefs. The Coral Reef Conservation Act of 2000 is scheduled for reauthorization in 2007.

The Proposed Action and other alternatives are consistent with the spirit and intent of these policies. Jarvis is one of only a few Federal no-take marine protected areas in the equatorial Pacific. Implementation of the Proposed Action would materially improve surveillance and enforcement and discourage unauthorized take of fish and wildlife within the refuge and improve the capacity of the Service to monitor fish and wildlife and manage their protection within the refuge.

_____   _____
Chief, Branch of Refuge Planning   Date